At Issue

Is Global Warming a Threat?

Other books in the At Issue series:

At Issue

Is Global Warming a Threat?

David M. Haugen and Susan Musser, Book Editors

GREENHAVEN PRESS

An imprint of Thomson Gale, a part of The Thomson Corporation

Detroit • New York • San Francisco • New Haven, Conn. • Waterville, Maine • London

THOMSON

✴ ™

GALE

Christine Nasso, *Publisher*
Elizabeth Des Chenes, *Managing Editor*

© 2007 The Gale Group.

For more information, contact:
Greenhaven Press
27500 Drake Rd.
Farmington Hills, MI 48331-3535
Or you can visit our Internet site at http://www.gale.com

LIBRARY OF CONGRESS CATALOGING-IN-PUBLICATION DATA

Is global warming a threat? / David M. Haugen and Susan Musser, book editors.
    p. cm. -- (At issue)
  Includes bibliographical references and index.
  ISBN-13: 978-0-7377-3687-8 (hardcover)
  ISBN-13: 978-0-7377-3688-5 (pbk.)
  1. Global warming--Juvenile literature. 2. Global warming--Environmental aspects--Juvenile literature. I. Haugen, David M., 1969- II. Musser, Susan
  QC981.8.G56I775 2008
  363.738'74--dc22

2007020044

ISBN-10: 0-7377-3687-9 (hardcover)
ISBN-10: 0-7377-3688-7 (pbk.)

Printed in the United States of America
10 9 8 7 6 5 4 3 2 1

Contents

Introduction

In May 2006 the film *An Inconvenient Truth* opened in Los Angeles and New York. This documentary about climate change was directed by Davis Guggenheim and features former vice president Al Gore discussing the damaging impact of global warming on the world's environment. Gore, presenting data and images in what has come to be known as his "slide show," describes how carbon dioxide (CO_2) and other gases generated primarily by fossil-fuel consumption have been spewed into the atmosphere where they trap heat close to the earth's surface. The heat comes from solar energy that would ideally be absorbed by the oceans and the land and then radiated back into space. The presence of heat-trapping gases such as CO_2, water vapor, and nitrous oxide, however, partially blocks the release of the earth's heat. The resulting "greenhouse effect" warms up the planet's temperature. In fact, scientists record that within the last century, global temperatures have risen roughly three-quarters of a degree Celsius. Extrapolating from this observation, Gore predicts that unchecked global warming will raise temperatures to destructive heights in the future, drying out soils, altering ecosystems, and melting polar ice that will subsequently swamp coastlines as the sea level rises. He warns that unless the world's governments and citizens take corrective steps to limit the emission of greenhouse gases, Earth is headed for catastrophe.

Critical response to *An Inconvenient Truth* was overwhelmingly positive, and several environmental organizations and publications support Gore's call to action. Writing in a 2006 edition of *Alternatives Journal*, Anita Krajnc, Larry Wartel, and Kellee A. Jacobs claim, "Nowhere is the quest for truth stronger, nor has a more cohesive case ever been made about the environmental crisis than in Al Gore's documentary on climate change." Gene Karpinski, the president of the League of

Conservation Voters, remarked, "With its eye-opening images and compelling storyline, this film helped jump start not only the current debate on global warming solutions in the presidential primary process, but in Congressional hearing rooms, board rooms and living rooms across the country and around the world." Indeed, in January 2007 the Senate Environment and Public Works Committee began hearings to gauge the views of senators on global warming in hopes that the policies maintained under President George W. Bush might be emended to strengthen the nation's commitment to averting crisis. At the same time, in the other house of Congress, the House Committee on Oversight and Government Reform was examining allegations that the Bush administration, which opposes mandatory cuts to greenhouse gas emissions, had suppressed climatology reports from government scientists in order to downplay the threat of global warming. These congressional activities as well as a host of magazine articles and Internet blog entries attest to the fact that climate change is currently one of the most pressing topics in the nation.

Not everyone, however, views *An Inconvenient Truth* and the spiking of interest in global warming as an urgent call worth answering. Senate Environment and Public Works Committee chairman James M. Inhofe (R-Okla.) refers to the investigation into the Bush administration as "purely eleventh-hour election-year politics." Inhofe is an outspoken critic of global warming who has dubbed the phenomenon a hoax. He argues that the warming of the planet is a natural response to the cooling trend that kept temperatures down through a period extending from the sixteenth century to the mid-nineteenth century. If planetary heating was due to buildup of CO_2, he asserts, then it is inexplicable why the warming trend began around 1850 when the atmosphere could not have yet responded to the impact of large-scale fossil-fuel burning. Inhofe and others have challenged the notion that the earth's warming and cooling is anything other than natural phenomena connected to changes in the sun's output and the movement of the planet through space. In applying this criticism to his review of *An Inconvenient Truth* for *Human Events* magazine, Roy W. Spencer questioned how Gore could blame fiercer storms, flood, drought, and even the melting of polar ice on global warming when "everything shown in the movie was, of course, happening even before global warming became popular."

When asked if he would see the Gore documentary, President Bush replied, "Doubt it" and then stated that "We need to set aside whether or not greenhouse gases have been caused by mankind or because of natural effects and focus on the technologies that will enable us to live better lives and at the same time protect the environment." The president has focused a part of his administrative policies on championing alternative energies to reduce the nation's oil dependency, the burning of which contributes to carbon dioxide emissions. He has also acknowledged that greenhouse gas emissions are a problem for the United States. However, the president has been reluctant to cut emissions because of potential harm to the economy. He has come under fire for not approving the Kyoto Protocol, an international agreement that sets caps on carbon dioxide emissions, because his administration maintains that the treaty allows developing nations to produce more CO_2 than industrialized nations, giving the developing countries unfair manufacturing benefits while providing them with less incentive to cut dangerous emissions. He contends that the United States will continue to work bilaterally with other nations to reduce greenhouse gas emissions through agreements and technological assistance. At home, the Bush administration is also committed to National Climate Change Technology Initiative, which funds universities and national labs that work to understand climate change and develop low-pollution, fuel-efficient energy sources.

Despite the Bush administration's environmental ventures, the president's reticence to address global warming as a national and universal issue has many people concerned. Al Gore told the Associated Press that the president's comments made in response to *An Inconvenient Truth* exemplified Bush's "personal doubt that [human-induced global warming] is true," which Gore believes makes the rest of the world suspicious of America's commitment to the problem. In 2004 the British newspaper the *Independent* even ran a headline that blared "US Climate Policy Bigger Threat to World than Terrorism." To some, such a statement underscores the grave consequences that will follow inattention to a global issue of deadly proportions, but to others, the hyperbole reflects unfounded alarmism. Whether or not such an accusation is warranted remains the subject of a debate that involves science, politics, and public opinion. In *At Issue: Is Global Warming a Threat?* commentators, legislators, scientists, and pundits demonstrate that global warming is a topic that spans morality and science, and perhaps more importantly, it is an issue that is far from resolved.

1

Global Warming Will Have Noticeable Local Impact

Roger Di Silvestro

Roger Di Silvestro is a senior editor of National Wildlife *magazine and the author of several books including* The Endangered Kingdom: The Struggle to Save America's Wildlife.

Though many people are tempted to think of global warming in terms of large-scale climatic changes that spell disaster for coastlines and rain forests, the consequences of a warming planet will also be evident in other communities across the globe. Wild plants that thrive on heat and high carbon dioxide concentrations will spread greatly. This will, in turn, increase the pollen count, aggravating human allergies. In addition, the hot weather will dry up soils and contribute to the breeding of larger, more active insect populations. Such irksome problems may become commonplace for nearly everyone living in moderate and hot climates if global warming remains unchecked.

If you're accustomed to thinking of global warming as something happening out there—say, in the Arctic or the Antarctic or high in the atmosphere—you may be in for a shock. Recent scientific studies indicate that global warming is likely soon to sneak into your backyard in the guise of burgeoning numbers of disease-carrying insects, escalating amounts of hay-fever-inducing pollen and faster growing and more toxic poison ivy. And it's not just your backyard that will be affected. You're likely to find that your dinner table feels the heat, too.

Roger Di Silvestro, "Global Warming: Coming to Your Backyard," *National Wildlife*, vol. 45, February–March 2007, pp. 14–17. Copyright 2007 National Wildlife Federation. Reproduced by permission.

Global warming is caused by a buildup of atmospheric gases increasingly emitted by human activities—mostly the burning of fossil fuels. Most prominent among these gases is carbon dioxide (CO_2), used by plants in photosynthesis, the process by which they turn sunlight into vegetable energy. Given the critical link between plants and CO_2, it makes sense that scientists would study how higher levels of the gas will affect plants. What they are finding is a warning to us all.

Spread of Invasive Plants

Consider woody vines, such as Japanese honeysuckle, kudzu, English ivy and other invasive plants that climb backyard fences and trees throughout the nation. In a [2006] study done in North Carolina, Duke University biologists used pipes to pump carbon dioxide into circular areas of forest, each about 100 feet in diameter. The biologists raised the CO_2 in the air to the level anticipated for our atmosphere by 2050 if CO_2 emissions continue unchanged—about 585 parts per million, "a level never before reached in all of human history," says William Schlesinger, dean of the Nicholas School of the Environment and Earth Sciences at Duke University. Presently, atmospheric CO_2 is at about 372 parts per million, the highest concentration in at least 420,000 years, as indicated by studies of gases trapped in ancient ice.

Increased plant growth suggests increased pollen production, unwelcome news to hay fever victims.

After five years of experimenting, biologists found that one woody vine—poison ivy—under increased CO_2 grew at two and a half times its normal rate. More ominously, the ivy produced a more powerful version of urushiol, the chemical that causes a rash in some 80 percent of people who come in contact with the plant, producing more than 350,000 reported U.S. cases of blistered skin yearly.

The researchers also concluded that other woody vines would enjoy the same rampant growth. Consequently, climbing vines such as honeysuckle may strangle and even topple trees, changing the face of the nation's forests and woody backyards, Schlesinger says.

Increased plant growth suggests increased pollen production, unwelcome news to hay fever victims, because that pollen will lead to an "appreciable increase in hay fever and asthma, which should alarm us all," Schlesinger says. A Harvard study released [in 2006] found that ragweed pollen production increased 55 percent under increased levels of CO_2. Another study, conducted by the University of Oklahoma between 1999 and 2001, found that in tall-grass prairie plots in which temperature was artificially raised, ragweed pollen production grew 84 percent. Considering that a single ragweed plant under current conditions can release up to a billion pollen grains in one season, for a nationwide annual ragweed pollen production of an estimated 100 million tons, these increases are formidable. In the Duke CO_2 studies, Schlesinger says, pines increased pollen production up to threefold, another escalating threat to hay fever victims.

Global warming researchers have predicted for years that the interior regions of continents will become drier as temperature rises.

Increased Insect Populations

Insects, too, are likely to be invigorated by warmer climates. "Long, cold winters have the potential to smack back insect populations," Schlesinger says. The shorter, warmer winters resulting from global warming could lead to more insects, he says, including disease-carrying mosquitoes. A warmer world is also likely to produce more robust tick populations, compounding the threat ticks pose as carriers of Lyme disease.

The Union of Concerned Scientists, on its website, reports that insects typical of southern parts of the United States are likely to shift north as climate warms. One insect that already appears to be moving north is the bean leaf beetle, which feeds on soybeans and carries a virus that causes disease in soybeans. Another likely to make the shift is the corn ear-worm, one of the most destructive crop pests in North America, a threat to a wide variety of crops, from corn to cabbage to eggplants and tomatoes. Presently, it cannot survive most winters north of Kansas and Virginia. It does reach as far north as Canada in summer, but generally too late to cause extensive damage. If warmer winters allow it to live year-round in more northerly areas, it will pose a greater threat to crops. To combat such pests, farmers are likely to use more pesticides, further jeopardizing the health of rivers and streams.

Crop Problems

Bruce Hungate, a climate ecologist and professor of biological sciences at Northern Arizona University, notes a more subtle effect of global warming: Studies in Florida show that faster plant growth produces a decline in plant nutritional value. As a result, insects have to eat more plant matter to get the same amount of nutrients. Gardeners thus may find themselves fighting an escalating war against increased numbers of back-yard insect pests, each seeking a greater amount of plant food. Crop plants also lose nutrient value as atmospheric CO_2 increases, Hungate says. He points, for example, to a study in Japan which found that the nutritional value of rice declined with more atmospheric CO_2.

In addition, the regions in which crops grow may change. In a study published [2006] in the Proceedings of the National Academy of Sciences, scientists predict an 80 percent drop in U.S. production of high-quality wine grapes because of a higher frequency of extremely hot days. "In a nutshell, extreme heat could wipe out many areas of high-quality wine production in the U.S.," Hungate says.

Global warming researchers have predicted for years that the interior regions of continents will become drier as temperature rises. This change could make the American Midwest less suitable for corn and wheat, while Canada may become more productive. "If I were a farmer in Saskatchewan or Manitoba, I'd be thinking this global warming might not be all bad," Schlesinger says. "If I were a farmer in Iowa, I'd be thinking about a change in life."

Under the effects of global warming, U.S. corn crop yields could drop by as much as 42 percent, according to figures from the Environmental Protection Agency (EPA). The news isn't all bad: Soybean crops could actually increase by up to 15 percent, depending on the specific effects of global warming on precipitation and other factors. On the other hand, soybeans also could decline by as much as 46 percent, according to EPA warnings.

Such shifts in regions of crop production, with increases in transportation costs, could change the price of foods ranging from breakfast cereals to donuts to bread.

2

Global Warming Is Media-Hyped Hysteria

James M. Inhofe

U.S. senator James M. Inhofe is a Republican from Oklahoma. He is a former chairman of the Senate Committee on Environment and Public Works, and has remained a professed skeptic of climate change due to human-induced global warming.

For years, environmental alarmists have asserted that the earth is heating up due to human activity—especially the releasing of carbon emissions. Few have made the keen observation that the earth is warming naturally as it overcomes the effects of the Little Ice Age that had plagued the globe until the mid-nineteenth century. Instead, the hysteria over runaway global warming has become an entrenched belief, and it has been reinforced by an unenlightened media that whole heartedly swallows environmentalist fears. Fortunately, the biased media organs preaching disaster cannot fool the people forever as more scientists step forward to point out the flaws of global warming theories.

I am going to speak today about the most media-hyped environmental issue of all time, global warming. I have spoken more about global warming than any other politician in Washington today. My speech will be a bit different from the previous seven [Senate] floor speeches, as I focus not only on the science, but on the media's coverage of climate change.

Global Warming—just that term evokes many members in this chamber, the media, Hollywood elites and our pop cul-

James M. Inhofe, "Inhofe to Blast Global Warming Media Coverage in Speech Today," U.S. Senate press release, September 25, 2006.

ture to nod their heads and fret about an impending climate disaster. As the senator who has spent more time educating about the actual facts about global warming, I want to address some of the recent media coverage of global warming and Hollywood's involvement in the issue. And of course I will also discuss former Vice President Al Gore's movie "An Inconvenient Truth."

Fluctuating Theories

Since 1895, the media has alternated between global cooling and warming scares during four separate and sometimes overlapping time periods. From 1895 until the 1930's the media peddled a coming ice age.

From the late 1920's until the 1960's they warned of global warming. From the 1950's until the 1970's they warned us again of a coming ice age. This makes modern global warming the fourth estate's fourth attempt to promote opposing climate change fears during the last 100 years.

Recently, advocates of alarmism have grown increasingly desperate to try to convince the public that global warming is the greatest moral issue of our generation. [In mid-September 2006], the vice president of London's Royal Society sent a chilling letter to the media encouraging them to stifle the voices of scientists skeptical of climate alarmism. During the past year, the American people have been served up an unprecedented parade of environmental alarmism by the media and entertainment industry, which link every possible weather event to global warming. The year 2006 saw many major organs of the media dismiss any pretense of balance and objectivity on climate change coverage and instead crossed squarely into global warming advocacy.

The Hockey Stick Fallacy

First, I would like to summarize some of the recent developments in the controversy over whether or not humans have created a climate catastrophe. One of the key aspects that the

United Nations, environmental groups and the media have promoted as the "smoking gun" of proof of catastrophic global warming is the so-called "hockey stick" temperature graph by climate scientist Michael Mann and his colleagues.

This graph purported to show that temperatures in the Northern Hemisphere remained relatively stable over 900 years, then spiked upward in the 20th century presumably due to human activity. Mann, who also co-publishes a global warming propaganda blog reportedly set up with the help of an environmental group, had his "Hockey Stick" come under severe scrutiny.

The "hockey stick" was completely and thoroughly broken once and for all in 2006. Several years ago, two Canadian researchers tore apart the statistical foundation for the hockey stick. In 2006, both the National Academy of Sciences and an independent researcher further refuted the foundation of the "hockey stick."

Alarmists fail to adequately explain why temperatures began warming at the end of the Little Ice Age in about 1850, long before man-made CO_2 emissions could have impacted the climate.

The National Academy of Sciences report reaffirmed the existence of the Medieval Warm Period from about 900 A.D. to 1300 A.D. and the Little Ice Age from about 1500 to 1850. Both of these periods occurred long before the invention of the SUV [sport-utility vehicle] or human industrial activity could have possibly impacted the Earth's climate. In fact, scientists believe the Earth was warmer than today during the Medieval Warm Period, when the Vikings grew crops in Greenland.

Climate alarmists have been attempting to erase the inconvenient Medieval Warm Period from the Earth's climate history for at least a decade. David Deming, an assistant professor at the University of Oklahoma's College of Geosciences, can testify first hand about this effort.

Dr. Deming was welcomed into the close-knit group of global warming believers after he published a paper in 1995 that noted some warming in the 20th century. Deming says he was subsequently contacted by a prominent global warming alarmist and told point blank "We have to get rid of the Medieval Warm Period." When the "Hockey Stick" first appeared in 1998, it did just that.

Natural Warming Follows Little Ice Age

The media have missed the big pieces of the puzzle when it comes to the Earth's temperatures and mankind's carbon dioxide (CO_2) emissions. It is very simplistic to feign horror and say the one degree Fahrenheit temperature increase during the 20th century means we are all doomed. First of all, the one degree Fahrenheit rise coincided with the greatest advancement of living standards, life expectancy, food production and human health in the history of our planet. So it is hard to argue that the global warming we experienced in the 20th century was somehow negative or part of a catastrophic trend.

Second, what the climate alarmists and their advocates in the media have continued to ignore is the fact that the Little Ice Age, which resulted in harsh winters which froze New York Harbor and caused untold deaths, ended about 1850. So trying to prove man-made global warming by comparing the well-known fact that today's temperatures are warmer than during the Little Ice Age is akin to comparing summer to winter to show a catastrophic temperature trend.

In addition, something that the media almost never addresses are the holes in the theory that CO_2 has been the driving force in global warming. Alarmists fail to adequately explain why temperatures began warming at the end of the Little Ice Age in about 1850, long before man-made CO_2 emissions could have impacted the climate. Then about 1940, just as man-made CO_2 emissions rose sharply, the temperatures began a decline that lasted until the 1970's, prompting the media and many scientists to fear a coming ice age. Let me repeat, temperatures got colder after CO_2 emissions exploded. If CO_2 is the driving force of global climate change, why do so many in the media ignore the many skeptical scientists who cite these rather obvious inconvenient truths?

The history of the modern environmental movement is chock full of predictions of doom that never came true.

My skeptical views on man-made catastrophic global warming have only strengthened as new science comes in. There have been recent findings in peer-reviewed literature over the last few years showing that the Antarctic is getting colder and the ice is growing and a new study in Geophysical Research Letters found that the sun was responsible for 50% of 20th century warming.

Recently, many scientists, including a leading member of the Russian Academy of Sciences, predicted long-term global cooling may be on the horizon due to a projected decrease in the sun's output. . . .

One final point on the science of climate change: I am approached by many in the media and others who ask, "What if you are wrong to doubt the dire global warming predictions? Will you be able to live with yourself for opposing the Kyoto Protocol?"

My answer is blunt. The history of the modern environmental movement is chock full of predictions of doom that never came true. We have all heard the dire predictions about the threat of overpopulation, resource scarcity, mass starvation, and the projected death of our oceans. None of these predictions came true, yet it never stopped the doomsayers from continuing to predict a dire environmental future.

The more the eco-doomsayers' predictions fail, the more the eco-doomsayers predict. These failed predictions are just one reason I respect the serious scientists out there today debunking the latest scaremongering on climate change. . . .

The Media Cannot Keep Their Story Straight

Many in the media, as I noted earlier, have taken it upon themselves to drop all pretense of balance on global warming and instead become committed advocates for the issue.

Here is a quote from *Newsweek* magazine: "There are ominous signs that the Earth's weather patterns have begun to change dramatically and that these changes may portend a drastic decline in food production with serious political implications for just about every nation on Earth."

A headline in the *New York Times* reads: "Climate Changes Endanger World's Food Output."

Here is a quote from *Time* Magazine: "As they review the bizarre and unpredictable weather pattern of the past several years, a growing number of scientists are beginning to suspect that many seemingly contradictory meteorological fluctuations are actually part of a global climatic upheaval."

All of this sounds very ominous. That is, until you realize that the three quotes I just read were from articles in 1975 editions of *Newsweek* Magazine and the *New York Times*, and *Time* Magazine in 1974.

They weren't referring to global warming; they were warning of a coming ice age.

Let me repeat, all three of those quotes were published in the 1970's and warned of a coming ice age.

In addition to global cooling fears, *Time* Magazine has also reported on global warming. Here is an example: "[Those] who claim that winters were harder when they were boys are quite right. . . weathermen have no doubt that the world at least for the time being is growing warmer."

Before you think that this is just another example of the media promoting [former] Vice President Gore's movie, you need to know that the quote I just read you from *Time* Magazine was not a recent quote; it was from January 2, 1939.

Yes, in 1939. Nine years before Vice President Gore was born and over three decades before *Time* Magazine began hyping a coming ice age and almost five decades before they returned to hyping global warming.

Time Magazine in 1951 pointed to receding permafrost in Russia as proof that the planet was warming.

In 1952, the *New York Times* noted that the "trump card" of global warming "has been the melting glaciers."

There are many more examples of the media and scientists flip-flopping between warming and cooling scares. . . .

Media Predictions Should Inspire Skepticism

These past predictions of doom have a familiar ring, don't they? They sound strikingly similar to our modern media promotion of [the] former vice president's brand of climate alarmism.

After more than a century of alternating between global cooling and warming, one would think that this media history would serve a cautionary tale for today's voices in the media and scientific community who are promoting yet another round of eco-doom. . . .

Which raises the question: Has this embarrassing 100-year documented legacy of coverage on what turned out to be trendy climate science theories made the media more skeptical of today's sensational promoters of global warming? You be the judge.

On February 19th of [2006], CBS News's "60 Minutes" produced a segment on the North Pole. The segment was a completely one-sided report, alleging rapid and unprecedented melting at the polar cap. It even featured correspondent Scott

Pelley claiming that the ice in Greenland was melting so fast, that he barely got off an ice-berg before it collapsed into the water.

"60 Minutes" failed to inform its viewers that a 2005 study by a scientist named Ola Johannessen and his colleagues showing that the interior of Greenland is gaining ice and mass and that according to scientists, the Arctic was warmer in the 1930's than today.

On March 19th of this year "60 Minutes" profiled NASA [National Aeronautics and Space Administration] scientist and alarmist James Hansen, who was once again making allegations of being censored by the [George W.] Bush administration. In this segment, objectivity and balance were again tossed aside in favor of a one-sided glowing profile of Hansen.

The "60 Minutes" segment made no mention of Hansen's partisan ties to former Democrat Vice President Al Gore or Hansen's receiving of a grant of a quarter of a million dollars from the left-wing Heinz Foundation run by Teresa Heinz Kerry. There was also no mention of Hansen's subsequent endorsement of her husband John Kerry for President in 2004.

Many in the media dwell on any industry support given to so-called climate skeptics, but the same media completely fail to note Hansen's huge grant from the left-wing Heinz Foundation. . . .

"60 Minutes" also did not inform viewers that Hansen appeared to concede in a 2003 issue of *Natural Science* that the use of "extreme scenarios" to dramatize climate change "may have been appropriate at one time" to drive the public's attention to the issues.

Unbalanced Views

Why would "60 Minutes" ignore the basic tenets of journalism, which call for objectivity and balance in sourcing, and do such one-sided segments?

The answer was provided by correspondent Scott Pelley. Pelley told the CBS News website that he justified excluding scientists skeptical of global warming alarmism from his segments because he considers skeptics to be the equivalent of "Holocaust deniers."

This year also saw a *New York Times* reporter write a children's book entitled "The North Pole Was Here." The author of the book, *New York Times* reporter Andrew Revkin, wrote that it may someday be "easier to sail to than stand on" the North Pole in summer. So here we have a very prominent environmental reporter for the *New York Times* who is promoting aspects of global warming alarmism in a book aimed at children.

In April of this year [2006], *Time* Magazine devoted an issue to global warming alarmism titled "Be Worried, Be Very Worried." This is the same *Time* Magazine which first warned of a coming ice age in the 1920's before switching to warning about global warming in the 1930's before switching yet again to promoting the 1970's coming ice age scare.

The April 3, 2006 global warming special report of *Time* Magazine was a prime example of the media's shortcomings, as the magazine cited partisan left-wing environmental groups with a vested financial interest in hyping alarmism.

Headlines blared:

"More and More Land is Being Devastated by Drought"

"Earth at the Tipping Point"

"The Climate is Crashing,"

Time Magazine did not make the slightest attempt to balance its reporting with any views with scientists skeptical of this alleged climate apocalypse.

I don't have journalism training, but I dare say calling a bunch of environmental groups with an obvious fund-raising agenda and asking them to make wild speculations on how bad global warming might become, is nothing more than advocacy for their left-wing causes. It is a violation of basic journalistic standards. . . .

Gore's Inconvenient Truth

In May, our nation was exposed to perhaps one of the slickest science propaganda films of all time: former Vice President Gore's "An Inconvenient Truth." In addition to having the backing of Paramount Pictures to market this film, Gore had the full backing of the media, and leading the cheerleading charge was none other than the Associated Press [AP].

On June 27, the Associated Press ran an article by Seth Borenstein that boldly declared "Scientists give two thumbs up to Gore's movie." The article quoted only five scientists praising Gore's science, despite AP's having contacted over 100 scientists.

The fact that over 80% of the scientists contacted by the AP had not even seen the movie or that many scientists have harshly criticized the science presented by Gore did not dissuade the news outlet one bit from its mission to promote Gore's brand of climate alarmism.

I am almost at a loss as to how to begin to address the series of errors, misleading science and unfounded speculation that appear in the former Vice President's film

Here is what Richard Lindzen, a meteorologist from MIT [Massachusetts Institute of Technology] has written about "An Inconvenient Truth."

"A general characteristic of Mr. Gore's approach is to ignore the fact that the earth and its climate are dynamic; they are always changing even without any external forcing. To treat all change as something to fear is bad enough; to do so in order to exploit that fear is much worse."

What follows is a very brief summary of the science that the former Vice President promotes in either a wrong or misleading way:

- He promoted the now debunked "hockey stick" temperature chart in an attempt to prove man's overwhelming impact on the climate.

- He attempted to minimize the significance of Medieval Warm period and the Little Ice Age.

- He insisted on a link between increased hurricane activity and global warming that most scientists believe does not exist.

- He asserted that today's Arctic is experiencing unprecedented warmth while ignoring that temperatures in the 1930's were as warm or warmer.

- He claimed the Antarctic was warming and losing ice but failed to note, that is only true of a small region and the vast bulk has been cooling and gaining ice.

- He hyped unfounded fears that Greenland's ice is in danger of disappearing.

- He erroneously claimed that the ice cap on Mt. Kilimanjaro [in Tanzania], is disappearing due to global warming, even while the region cools and researchers blame the ice loss on local land-use practices.

- He made assertions of massive future sea level rise that is way outside of any supposed scientific "consensus" and is not supported in even the most alarmist literature.

- He incorrectly implied that a Peruvian glacier's retreat is due to global warming, while ignoring the fact that the region has been cooling since the 1930s and other glaciers in South America are advancing.

- He blamed global warming for water loss in Africa's Lake Chad, despite NASA scientists concluding that local population and grazing factors are the more likely culprits.

- He inaccurately claimed polar bears are drowning in significant numbers due to melting ice when in fact they are thriving.

- He completely failed to inform viewers that the 48 scientists who accused President Bush of distorting science were part of a political advocacy group set up to support Democrat Presidential candidate John Kerry in 2004.

Now that was just a brief sampling of some of the errors presented in "An Inconvenient Truth." Imagine how long the list would have been if I had actually seen the movie—there would not be enough time to deliver this speech today....

Some Welcome Resistance

It is an inconvenient truth that so far, 2006 has been a year in which major segments of the media have given up on any quest for journalistic balance, fairness and objectivity when it comes to climate change. The global warming alarmists and their friends in the media have attempted to smear scientists who dare question the premise of man-made catastrophic global warming, and as a result some scientists have seen their reputations and research funding dry up.

The media has so relentlessly promoted global warming fears that a British group called the Institute for Public Policy Research—and this from a left leaning group—issued a report in 2006 accusing media outlets of engaging in what they termed "climate porn" in order to attract the public's attention.

Bob Carter, a Paleoclimate geologist from James Cook University in Australia has described how the media promotes climate fear: "Each such alarmist article is larded with words such as 'if', 'might', 'could', 'probably', 'perhaps', 'expected', 'projected' or 'modeled'—and many involve such deep dreaming, or ignorance of scientific facts and principles, that they are akin to nonsense," professor Carter concluded in an op-ed in April of this year.

Another example of this relentless hype is the reporting on the seemingly endless number of global warming impact studies which do not even address whether global warming is going to happen. They merely project the impact of potential temperature increases.

The American people know when their intelligence is being insulted. They know when they are being used and when they are being duped by the hysterical left.

The media endlessly hypes studies that purportedly show that global warming could increase mosquito populations, malaria, West Nile Virus, heat waves and hurricanes, threaten the oceans, damage coral reefs, boost poison ivy growth, damage vineyards, and global food crops, to name just a few of the global warming linked calamities.

Oddly, according to the media reports, warmer temperatures almost never seem to have any positive effects on plant or animal life or food production.

Fortunately, the media's addiction to so-called 'climate porn' has failed to seduce many Americans.

According to a July Pew Research Center Poll, the American public is split about evenly between those who say global warming is due to human activity versus those who believe it's from natural factors or not happening at all. This is down from 85 percent just a year ago.

In addition, an August *Los Angeles Times*/Bloomberg poll found that most Americans do not attribute the cause of recent severe weather events to global warming, and the portion of Americans who believe global warming is naturally occurring is on the rise.

Yes—it appears that alarmism has led to skepticism.

The American people know when their intelligence is being insulted. They know when they are being used and when they are being duped by the hysterical left. The American people deserve better—much better—from our fourth estate.

3

Global Warming May Not Be Caused by Human Activity

Robert Royal

Robert Royal is the director of the Faith and Reason Institute, a Washington, D.C., think tank that analyzes global issues. He has written articles for many periodicals and has published several books including The Virgin and the Dynamo: The Use and Abuse of Religion in the Environment Debate.

Many who fear global warming blame the phenomenon on human causes such as the polluting of the atmosphere with carbon dioxide emissions. But the heating of the earth may not have anthropogenic origins. The earth has naturally warmed and cooled over time, and scientists have previously pointed to nonhuman culprits such as magnetic activity from the sun to explain these climate changes. As for terrestrial causes, high carbon dioxide concentrations in the atmosphere could be pinned to such natural events as volcanic eruptions. If nature is responsible for the warming climate, humankind should reassess how urgent the crisis is and how best to react to it before hastily condemning human industry and progress.

The most exasperating thing about humankind is not, as T.S. Eliot wrote, that we "cannot bear very much reality." It is the corollary: We can bear far too much unreality. I've

Robert Royal, "What to Make of the Year Without a Winter," *National Catholic Reporter*, February 2, 2007, Column 17. Copyright © The National Catholic Reporter Publishing Company, 115 E. Armour Blvd., Kansas City, MO 64111. All rights reserved. Reproduced by permission of *National Catholic Reporter*, www.natcath.org.

been reminded of that in this strangely warm winter here on the East Coast as I've seen news stories linking the unreasonably nice weather to human-caused (anthropogenic) global warming.

I do not know for certain whether anthropogenic warming is real, though I looked carefully at it for a book I wrote years ago. Neither do you. And neither do the scientists. Climate change involves many complexities and uncertain comparisons with events over geologic time. The carbon dioxide we generate must cause some effects, though what exactly calls for modesty. Yet I find unreality in both main camps that might have made even T.S. Eliot tear his hair.

Naturally Fluctuating Climate

To begin with, Mother Nature would not exactly qualify as a Republican or a Democrat. She does not seem entirely docile under free markets or government regulation. Nature has, all on its own, warmed and cooled faster than anything we've seen in the past century. If you think the Year Without a Winter is a sign of our evil addiction to oil what do you make of the geologic evidence that in the past 1.5 million years climate has multiple times turned New England temperatures to those of Miami in as little as 25 years? Just 9,000 years ago, at the end of the last Ice Age, the earth was four degrees warmer than today.

Then, there is 1816—the Year Without a Summer—still not entirely understood, but partly due to what scientists call the Dalton Minimum, a low cycle of solar magnetic activity, actually one of several in the period known as the Little Ice Age (1300s to 1900s), which followed the Medieval Optimum, when grapes grew in Nova Scotia—Vineland to the Vikings. Further, the sun seems to have moved, as it does in a roughly 180-year-long cycle, to a slightly different position within our solar system. But there was also—such coincidences often occur—volcanic eruption in Indonesia, which may have had worldwide effects. Volcanoes routinely emit sulfur dioxide and other pollutants at far higher than human levels.

Nature Is Not Benign

This, and much more of an astonishing and unpredictable character, is the nature God made. Now, this should not make anyone complacent about what we may be doing to creation. In spite of the irritation of some Republicans, the ecological movement has done some good. Water and air are cleaner than just a few decades ago. We pay more attention to preserving or restoring natural settings.

Half of what we call global warming occurred before the 1940s, prior to the anthropogenic buildup of carbon dioxide in the air.

But contrary to a certain kind of ecological enthusiast (there are conservatives, if not many Republicans, in this category), nature was not benign or even very stable prior to modern industrialized society. A few years ago an otherwise intelligent woman who occupies a chair at our most prestigious Catholic university told me during a conference sponsored by the American bishops that humans and nature were not at odds until greed entered the picture. It's a shame such persons cannot be in e-mail contact with our cave dwelling forbears or any number of people who fought droughts, famine, floods, epidemics, tsunamis or wild animals over the centuries.

A Prudent Response

We got into earlier trouble not out of greed. We just didn't realize our power as our industries and technologies grew in response to human needs. When we did, we took steps to correct them and succeeded in spite of corporate and political foot-draggers. But every environmental question deserves an appropriate response, which means we have to use our brains prudently. Though the earth is warming to a certain extent we need, as the statistician Bjorn Lomborg has shown, to assess the urgency of the problem. No family would, for example, spend all its resources on a new furnace or non-polluting car if other and greater needs also existed. Mr. Lomborg's careful statistical assessment is that many problems, including those of the world's poorest, are more pressing. Global warming's effects are likely manageable.

Prudence dictates that we take a calm and open-eyed approach. Half of what we call global warming occurred before the 1940s, prior to the anthropogenic buildup of carbon dioxide in the air. Nature was already moving in a direction that has nothing to do with us. From the middle of the century to the 1970s, there was unusually cold weather in the world, while the last quarter of a century has been unusually warm. Should we place a huge economic and human bet on the basis of this evidence?

Personally, I think it's wise to keep the question open. It may be a good idea on other grounds to reduce our consumption of fossil fuels and live simpler lives. For many people, this seems to be the underlying belief that makes them sympathetic to environmental extremism. For the rest of us, warming is one of several challenges. Our ancestors fought scarcity. We deal with problems of abundance. In a fallen world, that's only to be expected. But let's not add to the reality of our problems the unreality of overheated, hasty and unwise solutions.

4

Global Warming Will Be Beneficial

James S. Robbins

James S. Robbins is senior fellow in national security affairs at the American Foreign Policy Council and a trustee for the Leaders for Liberty Institute, an educational organization dedicated to advancing freedom worldwide. Robbins is also a professor of international relations at the School for National Security Executive Education at the National Defense University in Washington, D.C.

If global warming does exist—and there is significant skepticism—the heating of the earth would probably be a boon to the colder nations of the world. Ice-free land would allow for planting of crops and more areas for habitation. Though sea levels may rise and endanger the world's coastlines, humans have great ingenuity and could find ways to overcome and avert catastrophe. Global warming alarmism, then, is really the fear of change—and in this case, change would probably be beneficial.

Every time we have a summer heatwave invariably the media go crazy with talk of global warming. You would think they would be used to the phenomenon of seasons by now. But it is great fodder for the features producers, and since the weather is on everybody's mind you might as well go with a segment on climate change. It's a nice respite from the real problems in the world.

Personally, I don't know what all the shouting is about. Global warming is great. Granted, maybe it isn't really hap-

James S. Robbins, "Hooray for Global Warming," *National Review Online*, August 8, 2006. Reproduced by permission.

pening, and if it is there are strong reasons to doubt that humans have anything to do with it. But if the world is warming, I say "bravo." People in most parts of the globe should have no objection to a warmer, wetter climate. If the aliens were watching they'd conclude we were making our planet more habitable on purpose.

Consider the large landmasses in the northern hemisphere, say north of 55 degrees. These are very extreme climates for human habitation. A population distribution map of Canada shows most people live in a belt running along the southern border with the United States. But add global warming and vast regions would become comfortably habitable. As well, there would be more land available for cultivation. Resources would be easier to extract. True, there might be some dislocations as crops shifted northward, but so what? Economies change all the time. And imagine the land boom up the coastlines as people rushed on up for beachfront property. If global warming is real it is creating the investment opportunity of a lifetime.

A warmer wetter world could very well mean more rain forests—hence more biodiversity!

Shore Up the Shoreline

Of course, you have to factor in ice-cap melt and the possibility that today's shoreline might move inland. The Al Gore scare film [*An Inconvenient Truth*] has some dramatic footage of the consequences of a 20-foot rise in sea levels. Most estimates I have read about talk about a three-foot-rise at most, but let's not quibble. In the movie, oceans are seen rushing inland, implying some kind of inundation episode. But the waters will not rise so quickly, if they do at all. And if this threatens our cities one would think some form of sea wall would be in order. The Dutch have been doing this for years, there is no reason why we can't copy them.

And in response to Gore's grotesque pandering—saying that if sea levels rose high enough the Ground Zero site in New York would be under water—I say no, sir, we cannot, we will not let this happen! A wall I say! We will protect that sacred ground at all costs! No patriotic American, no real American, would settle for less! Anyway, get with it Democrats, where is your traditional love of public works? Rising ocean levels will keep the government in the sea wall business for decades.

In any case there is no compelling evidence that the seas are rising. The catastrophists warn that small islands and atolls will be the first to go, and the island state of Tuvalu in the Pacific has made a habit of demanding western aid as compensation for this imminent threat to their very existence. It plays well with the liberal guilt complex. But sea-level data from Tuvalu show basically a flat-line average since 1977—talk about an inconvenient truth!

Aiding Biodiversity

Think of the other advantages the Left is ignoring. A warmer wetter world could very well mean more rain forest—hence more biodiversity! We are supposed to value that for some reason, right? And if the ice caps melt and we get more ocean, well that just means more habitat for whales doesn't it? And warmer climates might reverse the migration pattern in this country away from the frigid liberal northeast towards the warm conservative south. Imagine Massachusetts and Vermont gaining seats in Congress and then tell me how bad global warming is.

Granted, there will be some negative impacts in marginal areas. Some rare plant and animal species, hyper-adapted to highly specific climate conditions or microbiotic zones, are already unable to cope with the change. Many may go extinct; some already have. That's tough, but chalk it up to bad evolutionary choices. When those rigidly specialist species bet everything on a small part of the world in hopes it would never change, they made a very bad bargain. For our part, we have air conditioners, lightweight fabrics, and sunscreen. Why infinitely adaptable humanity has to pay the price for the evolutionary shortsightedness of other life forms is beyond me.

Global warming is the latest in an endless line of apocalyptic scenarios that have captured the imaginations of the impressionable.

It seems to be beyond a lot of others too, because the public has yet to mobilize behind the movement to save the rare burrowing mountain toads of Central America. So the global-warming crowd started talking about polar bears drowning as their ice Arctic floes melted. Presumably this happens every summer to some of the more stupid ones, but regardless, it is a great marketing gimmick. Always tie in children, dogs and bears whenever possible, in anything you do.

Fear of Change

Basically I am questioning the premise of the global-warming alarmists, namely that this is a problem rather than an opportunity. And besides, I distrust their motives. Many are simply panicky people in need of some form of approaching eschatology [end of the world beliefs]. These sad folk afflicted with the "true believer" psychology require something large and threatening to worry about in order to give meaning to their lives. It could be anything—Y2K, Ebola virus, bird flu, overpopulation, technological meltdown—any event, trend, disease, or phenomenon which could, under certain implausible circumstances, lead to the end-of-the-world. People derive meaning from these things by being more in the know about this imminent doom than their ignorant neighbors, to whom they feel measurably superior, and whom they must protect from this looming catastrophe whether they like it or not.

Global warming is the latest in an endless line of apocalyptic scenarios that have captured the imaginations of the impressionable.

Another motive, sometimes open sometimes not, is to end the free-market system as we know it. By linking the cause of global warming to the activities of the most productive economies in human history, they can take down capitalism by other means. The analogous battle cry in the 1970s was "resource scarcity," the belief that the world was running out [of] oil, iron, water, cultivable land, or whatever; so in order to stave off the big crash, we had to move to immediate state controls over most human productive activity. Which leads to my third issue, which is that the solutions to the global-warming problem usually take the form of government regulations, restrictions, and of course massive wealth transfers to pay for the whole thing.

At the root of global-warming alarmism is a deathly fear of change. It is ironic that the Left, which calls itself progressive, is comprised of some of the most reactionary people on earth. They will come up with endless lists of all the changes that will result from temperature increases, exclusively focusing on the negative, as though change per se is something to be avoided.

But change is natural. Gaia [nature] is all about change. If the climate historians can tell us anything, it is that climatic conditions have been changing radically since Earth's creation, and there is no reason to expect that they will ever stop. Forget the idea that man is causing global warming—I think it is terribly ambitious to believe that man can stop it.

So if we see global warming for the beneficial trend that it is rather than a looming threat to life and limb, none of the "solutions" being proposed by the alarmists are necessary. There is no challenge posed by a slow-rolling phenomenon like global warming that cannot be overcome; and when deserts start blooming, blizzards stop hitting, and you are enjoying the surfing at your beach house in upper Newfoundland, you won't care what caused global warming, you'll just thank goodness it happened.

5

Global Warming Is Melting Polar Ice Masses

Natural Resources Defense Council

The Natural Resources Defense Council is a national environmental organization with more than one million members. It uses legal advocacy and activism to influence public policy and to inform the public about threats to the planet, its wildlife, and its natural resources.

As global warming raises temperatures on the earth, the frozen ice sheets of the Arctic are melting and rupturing. The melt is destroying habitats of arctic animals—such as the polar bear—and will likely swamp the native settlements that dot the region's coastline. The effects will also be felt worldwide. The melting ice will raise sea levels, flooding coastal areas, and the loss of cold arctic air fronts may jeopardize some crop yields.

1. *Why are global warming specialists watching the Arctic so closely?*

The Arctic is global warming's canary in the coal mine. It's a highly sensitive region, and it's being profoundly affected by the changing climate. Most scientists view what's happening now in the Arctic as a harbinger of things to come.

2. *What kinds of changes are taking place in the Arctic now?*

Average temperatures in the Arctic region are rising twice as fast as they are elsewhere in the world. Arctic ice is getting thinner, melting and rupturing. For example, the largest single block of ice in the Arctic, the Ward Hunt Ice Shelf, had been around for 3,000 years before it started cracking in 2000. Within two years it had split all the way through and is now breaking into pieces.

The polar ice cap as a whole is shrinking. Images from NASA [National Aeronautics and Space Administration] satellites show that the area of permanent ice cover is contracting at a rate of 9 percent each decade. If this trend continues, summers in the Arctic could become ice-free by the end of the century.

3. *How does this dramatic ice melt affect the Arctic?*

The melting of once-permanent ice is already affecting native people, wildlife and plants. When the Ward Hunt Ice Shelf splintered, the rare freshwater lake it enclosed, along with its unique ecosystem, drained into the ocean. Polar bears, whales, walrus and seals are changing their feeding and migration patterns, making it harder for native people to hunt them. And along Arctic coastlines, entire villages will be uprooted because they're in danger of being swamped. The native people of the Arctic view global warming as a threat to their cultural identity and their very survival.

A warmer Arctic will also affect weather patterns and thus food production around the world.

---

4. *Will Arctic ice melt have any effects beyond the polar region?*

Yes—the contraction of the Arctic ice cap is accelerating global warming. Snow and ice usually form a protective, cooling layer over the Arctic. When that covering melts, the earth absorbs more sunlight and gets hotter. And the latest scientific data confirm the far-reaching effects of climbing global temperatures.

Rising temperatures are already affecting Alaska, where the spruce bark beetle is breeding faster in the warmer weather.

These pests now sneak in an extra generation each year. From 1993 to 2003, they chewed up 3.4 million acres of Alaskan forest.

Melting glaciers and land-based ice sheets also contribute to rising sea levels, threatening low-lying areas around the globe with beach erosion, coastal flooding, and contamination of freshwater supplies. (Sea level is not affected when floating sea ice melts.) At particular risk are island nations like the Maldives [in the Indian Ocean]; over half of that nation's populated islands lie less than 6 feet above sea level. Even major cities like Shanghai [China] and Lagos [Nigeria] would face similar problems, as they also lie just six feet above present water levels.

Rising seas would severely impact the United States as well. Scientists project as much as a 3-foot sea-level rise by 2100. According to a 2001 U.S. Environmental Protection Agency study, this increase would inundate some 22,400 square miles of land along the Atlantic and Gulf coasts of the United States, primarily in Louisiana, Texas, Florida and North Carolina.

A warmer Arctic will also affect weather patterns and thus food production around the world. Wheat farming in Kansas, for example, would be profoundly affected by the loss of ice cover in the Arctic. According to a NASA Goddard Institute of Space Studies computer model, Kansas would be 4 degrees warmer in the winter without Arctic ice, which normally creates cold air masses that frequently slide southward into the United States. Warmer winters are bad news for wheat farmers, who need freezing temperatures to grow winter wheat. And in summer, warmer days would rob Kansas soil of 10 percent of its moisture, drying out valuable cropland.

5. *Can we do anything to stop global warming?*

Yes. When we burn fossil fuels—oil, coal and gas—to generate electricity and power our vehicles, we produce the heat-trapping gases that cause global warming. The more we burn, the faster chums the engine of global climate change. Thus the most important thing we can do is save energy.

And we *can* do it. Technologies exist today to make cars that run cleaner and burn less gas, generate electricity from wind and sun, modernize power plants, and build refrigerators, air conditioners and whole buildings that use less power. As individuals, each of us can take steps to save energy and fight global warming.

6

Polar Ice Masses Are Not Melting

Patrick Michaels

Patrick Michaels is a research professor of environmental sciences at the University of Virginia. He is also a senior fellow in environmental studies at the Cato Institute and a contributing author and reviewer of the United Nations Intergovernmental Panel on Climate Change.

Coastal catastrophes due to predicted global warming are often blamed on the resulting melting of polar ice and other ice concentrations in Greenland and around the world. Research has shown, however, that the Antarctic is experiencing high snowfalls, increasing the ice mass, and Greenland's loss or gain of ice is still uncertain. If these regions remain secure, sea levels could not rise significantly even if all other ice regions on the planet melted.

One of the great fears generated by global warming is that the ocean is about to rise and swallow our coasts. These concerns have been heightened by the substantial uptick in Atlantic hurricane activity that began in 1995. The frequency of really strong storms striking the U.S now resembles what it was in the 1940s and 50s, which few people (aging climatologists excepted) remember.

Those arguing that global warming is an overblown issue have been claiming for years that "consensus" forecasts of sea-

Patrick Michaels, "How Much Ice in the Global Cocktail?" *TCS Daily*, November 4, 2005. Copyright © 2005 Tech Central Station, www.techcentralstation.com. Reproduced by permission.

level are equally overwrought. The United Nations' [UN] Intergovernmental Panel on Climate Change predicts a global average rise of from 3.5 to 34 inches by 2100, with a central estimate of 19 inches. Depending upon how you slice or dice the data, the last century saw maybe six inches.

Critics have long argued that these changes require a substantial net melting of some combination of the world's two largest masses of land-based ice, Antarctica and Greenland. In addition, they note that observed global warming is right near the low end of the U.N.'s projections, which means that realized sea level rise should be similarly modest.

Studies Show Cooling Trends and More Snow

[In 1989] John Sansom published a paper in *Journal of Climate* that showed no net warming of Antarctica. While it was widely cited by critics of global warming doom, no one seemed to take notice. After all, it relied on only a handful of stations. Then, in 2002, Peter Doran published a more comprehensive analysis in *Nature* and found a cooling trend.

At the same time, a deluge of stories appeared, paradoxically, about Antarctic warming. These studies concentrated on the tip of the Antarctic Peninsula, the narrow strip of land that juts out towards South America. That region, which comprises less than one-half of one percent of Antarctica, is warming because the surrounding ocean has warmed.

Warmer water evaporates more moisture. The colder the land surface over which that moisture passes, the more it snows. So, Antarctica as a whole should gain snow and ice. [In 2004], C.H. Davis published a paper in *Science* about how this accumulating snowfall over East Antarctica was reducing sea level rise. This year, Duncan Wingham, at the 2005 Earth Observations summit in Brussels [Belgium], demonstrated the phenomenon is observed all over Antarctica.

Greenland is more complex. In 2000 William Krabill estimated the contribution of Greenland to sea level rise of 0.13 mm per year, or a half an inch per century. That's not very much ifferent than zero. In [October 2005] using satellite altimetry, O.M. Johannessen published a remarkable finding in *Science* that the trend in Greenland ice is a gain of 5.4 cm (two inches) per year.

It is simply impossible for the scientific community to ignore what is going on, even as prone to exaggeration of threats as it has grown to be.

Almost all of the gain in Greenland is for areas greater than 5000 feet in elevation (which is most of the place). Below that, there is glacial recession. It shouldn't be lost on anyone that because no one ventures into the hostile interior of Greenland, all we see are pictures of the receding glaciers near the coast!

The temperature situation in Greenland is more mixed than in Antarctica. Over the last 75 years, there's been cooling in the southern portion (where the recession is greatest) and some warming in the North.

Remaining Ice Melt Could Not Swamp Coasts

The only other masses of ice on the planet that can contribute to sea level rise arc the non-polar glaciers, but they are very few and far between. The biggest is the Himalayan ice cap, but it's so high that a substantial portion will always remain. Most of the rest are teeny objects tucked away in high elevation nooks and crannies, like our Glacier National Park [in Montana].

If all these glaciers melted completely—including the Himalayan ice cap—sea level could rise no more than five to seven inches, because there's just not that much mass of ice, compared to Antarctica and Greenland.

It is simply impossible for the scientific community to ignore what is going on, even as prone to exaggeration of threats as it has grown to be. The planet is warming at the low end of projections. Antarctica is undoubtedly gaining, not losing ice. Greenland appears to either lose a little ice, or, in [a 2005] study of Johannessen, gain dramatically. It's going to take some time for it to contribute much to rising oceans.

Meanwhile, Antarctica grows. Computer models, while still shaky, are now encountering reality, and every one of them now says that Antarctica contributes negatively to sea level rise in the next century, while almost every model now has Greenland's contribution as a few inches, at best.

It is inevitable that one of tomorrow's headlines will be that scientists have dramatically scaled back their projections of sea level rise associated with global warming. Had they paid attention to data (and snow) that began accumulating as long as fifteen years ago, they would have never made such outlandish forecasts to begin with.

7

Global Warming Is Contributing to Stronger Hurricanes

Mark Hertsgaard

An independent journalist, Mark Hertsgaard is the environment correspondent for the Nation *and the political correspondent for U.S. satellite broadcaster, LinkTV. He is also the author of* Earth Odyssey *and other nonfiction works.*

When Hurricane Katrina struck the Gulf Coast in August 2005, it should have been a wake-up call for those who still ignore the dangers of global warming. Although no one can point directly to a cause-and-effect relationship between Katrina and global warming, few scientists and observers doubt that continued emission of greenhouse gases will ensure that storms will only get more intense and destructive.

How many killer hurricanes will it take before America gets serious about global warming? It's hard to imagine a more clear-cut wake-up call than Hurricane Katrina: environmentally speaking, it was nearly the perfect storm. In a single catastrophic event, it brought together the most urgent environmental problem of our time—global warming—with the most telling but least acknowledged environmental truth: When the bill for our collective behavior comes due, it is invariably the non-white, nonaffluent members of society who pay a disproportionate share. And who said Mother Nature has no sense of irony? Katrina (and then Rita) struck at a ma-

Mark Hertsgaard, "Global Storm Warning," *Nation*, vol. 281, October 17, 2005, pp. 3, 5. Copyright © 2005 by The Nation Magazine/The Nation Company, Inc. Reproduced by permission of the author.

jor production site for America's oil and natural gas—the two carbon-based fuels that, along with coal, help drive global warming.

What's more, Katrina's primary target already ranked as the most environmentally ravaged state in the union. Louisiana is home to "Cancer Alley," a 100-mile stretch between New Orleans and Baton Rouge that contains the greatest concentration of petrochemical factories in the United States. Pollution from those factories has punished nearby communities—again, mainly poor and black—for decades, as Steve Lerner documented in his [2005] book *Diamond*. This pollution has also drained into the Mississippi River, where it joins fertilizer and pesticide runoff from millions of acres of Midwestern farmland to flow into the Gulf of Mexico, creating a massive "dead zone" off the Louisiana coast—1,400 square miles of ocean floor as bereft of life as an Arizona desert. The dead zone would be smaller except that Louisiana, like America as a whole, has lost a third of its coastal wetlands to economic development. Wetlands filter out impurities, much as the liver does for the human body. They also perform a second vital ecosystem function, acting as buffers that absorb and diminish the giant waves that hurricanes generate before they strike inland. Louisiana's loss of wetlands helps explain why the floods Katrina unleashed ended up overrunning 466 chemical factories, thirty-one Superfund [hazardous waste] sites and 500 sewage treatment plants, according to the *Times-Picayune* and the *Houston Chronicle*, leaving behind a toxic soup whose long-term health effects are incalculable.

A Wake-Up Call

Despite these horrors some leading environmentalists see a potential silver lining in Katrina: They believe it may finally awaken the United States from its environmental complacency, especially about global warming. "Sea-level rise and increased storm intensity are no longer abstract, long-term issues but are associated with horrific pictures seen on television every evening," says Christopher Flavin, president of the Worldwatch Institute.

Yes, the [George W.] Bush Administration and its right-wing allies will continue to deny that global warming exists and resist cutting carbon emissions. But global warming foot-draggers have succeeded in the past largely because the public was confused about whether the problem really existed. That confusion was encouraged by the mainstream media, which in the name of journalistic "balance" gave equal treatment to global warming skeptics and proponents alike, even though the skeptics represented a tiny fringe of scientific opinion and often were funded by companies with a financial interest in discrediting global warming. Katrina, however, may mark a turning point for the media as well as the public.

"The reaction has been more positive than any time in the sixteen years that I've been trying to make noise about global warming," says Bill McKibben, author of the 1989 classic *The End of Nature*. The day after Katrina hit, McKibben wrote an article for TomDispatch.com arguing that the devastation of New Orleans was, alas, only the first of many global warming disasters destined to strike in the twenty-first century. When McKibben appeared on radio shows to discuss the article, he says, "Everyone, and I mean everyone, who called in said, Thank heaven someone is saying this stuff, because it's what I'm thinking about all the time now."

Over time, humanity's loading of the climatic dice guarantees that there will be more killer hurricanes like Katrina.

"Had I said this stuff two years ago, the reactions would have ranged from skeptical to hostile, except for the liberal outlets," says Ross Gelbspan, whose Op-Ed article in the *Boston Globe* arguing that Katrina's "real name was global warming" led to forty-five media appearances. Gelbspan, who exposed industry funding of global warming skeptics in his book *The Heat Is On*, adds, "Even a couple of hostile, initially antagonistic right-wing talk-show hosts were drawn into the discussion—and their remarks turned from provocative to curious to sympathetic."

Few Doubt the Connection to Global Warming

"There aren't many reporters left who believe the skeptics," says Phil Clapp, president of the National Environmental Trust. Clapp credits the joint statement issued by eleven of the world's national academies of science (including America's), before last June's meeting of the G-8 nations [Canada, France, Germany, Italy, Japan, Russia, the United Kingdom, and the United States], declaring that global warming was a grave danger requiring immediate attention. "You may not have seen headlines screaming that Katrina was caused by global warming," Clapp adds, "but every reporter I've talked to has come to the position in their own mind that we have to prepare for global warming's effects."

But what journalists think in their own minds matters less than what they put on the air and in the papers. And given the gravity of the situation, screaming headlines are warranted. It's true that global warming can't be definitively blamed for one particular weather event; weather is the product of too many different factors to allow such specificity. Seizing on this fact, skeptics now trumpet scientific studies that portray Katrina as simply a manifestation of a natural long-term pattern in which first strong then weak hurricanes predominate. That pattern is real, but it doesn't invalidate global warming; the two trends can co-exist. The scientists at RealClimate.org offer a useful analogy: Imagine a set of dice loaded so that double sixes come up twice as often as normal. If the dice are then rolled and double sixes do come up, the loading may or may not be responsible for the result; after all, regular dice sometimes yield double sixes, too. All that's certain is that over time the frequency of double sixes will increase. Likewise, Katrina might have been an extra-powerful hurricane even if humanity had never emitted a single greenhouse gas. But over time, humanity's loading of the climatic dice guarantees that there will be more killer hurricanes like Katrina. We'd better get ready, and quickly.

8

There Is No Proven Link Between Global Warming and Hurricane Strength

Marlo Lewis Jr. and Iain Murray

Marlo Lewis Jr. and Iain Murray are senior fellows at the Competitive Enterprise Institute, a nonprofit public policy organization dedicated to advancing the principles of free enterprise and limited government. Both Lewis and Murray specialize in environmental topics including global warming and energy policy.

Global warming doomsayers predict that the heating of the planet's oceans will lead to more intense hurricanes, cyclones, and other storms. Science has suggested that an increase in global temperatures may affect storms, but no one can conclusively say how. Without a proven connection between global warming and storm strength, these warnings are unfounded. Assuredly, then, the United States should not base its energy policies on global warning alarmism.

One year on from Hurricane Katrina, the worst event of the intense hurricane season of 2005, environmental activists are using the hurricane's memory to promote their political agenda. For example, on August 9 [2006], Environmental Defense had this to say:

"Katrina-like events will become more common and more widespread unless the emissions of global warming pollut-

Marlo Lewis, Jr. and Iain Murray, "Katrina and Her Policy Waves," *Competitive Enterprise Institute: CEIn Point*, No. 107, August 28, 2006. Copyright © 2006 *Competitive Enterprise Institute*. Reproduced by permission.

ants are capped. The link between global warming and hurricanes is yet another reason for Americans to insist on meaningful legislation to cap our greenhouse gas emissions."

On August 20 [2006], in an emotional *Washington Post* op ed, Mike Tidwell of the self-styled "U.S. Climate Emergency Council" went further:

"Barring a rapid change in our nation's relationship to fossil fuels, every American within shouting distance of an ocean—including all of us in the nation's capital—will become de facto New Orleanians. Imagine a giant floodgate spanning the Potomac River just north of Mount Vernon [in Virginia], there to hold back the tsunami-like surge tide of the next great storm. Imagine the Mall, Reagan National Airport and much of Alexandria well below sea level, at the mercy of 'trust-us-they'll-hold' levees maintained by the Army Corps of Engineers. Imagine the rest of Washington [D.C.] vulnerable to the winds of major hurricanes that churn across a hot and swollen Chesapeake Bay, its surface free of the once vast and buffering wetland grasses and 'speed bump' islands that slow down storms."

These appeals share several factors: They depend on fear, they overstate the science, and they advance policy goals that will do little to protect vulnerable populations. In doing so, they represent an immoral exploitation of the victims of Katrina.

Exploiting Fears

Roger Pielke, Jr. of the University of Colorado, a leading researcher in the field of hurricane damage, compared Mr. Tidwell's article to something you might find in the *Weekly World News*. Tidwell's is an extreme example, but the Environmental Defense article and other popular treatments of global warming—such as former Vice President Al Gore's movie *An Inconvenient Truth*—all seek to persuade by exciting feelings *of alarm in their audience. And they rely on this argmentum ad mentum* (appeal to fear) fallacy because their central scientific argument is weak.

Claims of a definite link between hurricanes and global warming rely on the simple hypothesis that, as waters warm, storms get stronger. In fact, *some* storms *may* get stronger, but others may get weaker. There are two main types of storms: hurricanes (tropical cyclones) and winter (frontal) storms. Global warming is likely to affect each type differently.

Hurricanes draw their energy from the sea, and require warm sea surface temperatures (SSTs) to form. Some hurricanes may get stronger, and the area of hurricane formation may expand, as the oceans warm. However, once SSTs reach about 83°F, as routinely happens in the Gulf of Mexico every summer, any hurricane has the potential to become a major— Category 3, 4, or 5—storm, if other conditions are present. Such conditions include high humidity (dry air dissipates the hurricane's thunderstorm core) and low wind shear (strong winds in the upper troposphere rip hurricanes apart). Whether, or to what extent, global warming is actually increasing the strength or frequency—or both—of hurricanes is an empirical question, discussed below.

Winter storms draw their energy from the collision between cold and warm air fronts. If, as climate models predict, higher northern latitudes warm more than do lower tropical latitudes, the temperature differential between colliding air masses should decrease, reducing the intensity of some winter storms.

Scientists Do Not Agree on a Connection

Alarmists assert that there is a "scientific consensus" that global warming has been linked to an increase in the duration and intensity of hurricanes (Al Gore says as much in his movie *An Inconvenient Truth*). But the scientific jury is still out on these matters. Kerry Emanuel of MIT [Massachusetts Institute of Technology] found that hurricane strength, a combination of wind speed and storm duration, which he calls the "power dissipation index" (PDI), increased by 50 percent since the mid-1970s, and that the increase is highly correlated with rising SSTs. However, other experts question these results.

Alarmists also assert that there has been an increase in the frequency of the most damaging category 4 and 5 hurricanes. Again, the science here is in dispute.

The University of Colorado's Roger Pielke, Jr. finds that once hurricane damage is normalized for changes in population, wealth, and inflation, there is no long-term change in hurricane damage—which runs counter to the hypothesis that hurricanes are becoming more destructive. Christopher Landsea of the National Oceanic and Atmospheric Administration (NOAA), noting no trend in the PDI for land-falling U.S. hurricanes, suggests that Emanuel's finding may be an "artifact of the data"—a consequence of advances in satellite technology, which have improved detection, monitoring, and analysis of non-land-falling hurricanes.

Philip Klotzbach of Colorado State University found "a large increasing trend in tropical cyclonic intensity and longevity for the North Atlantic basin and a considerable decreasing trend for the North Pacific," but essentially no trend in other tropical cyclone-producing ocean basins.

The Accumulated Cyclone Energy (ACE) index is a measure of the energy contained in a tropical cyclone over its lifetime. From 1986 through 2005, there was an increase in the North Atlantic, a decrease in the Northeast Pacific, and not much long-term change anywhere else.

Even more problematic for climate alarmists, although there was a slight increase in ACE worldwide during 1986–2005, found a slight downward trend during 1990–2005, even though tropical sea surface temperatures increased by approximately 0.2°C to 0.3°C during this period. . . .

Alarmists also assert that there has been an increase in the frequency of the most damaging category 4 and 5 hurricanes. Again, the science here is in dispute. Peter Webster of Georgia Tech and colleagues found a significant increase in the number of major hurricanes during 1970–2004. In contrast, Philip J. Klotzbach of Colorado State University found only a "small increase in global Category 4–5 hurricanes from the period 1986–1995 to the period 1996–2005," and considers it likely that "improved observational technology" accounts for the small increase he observed.

University of Virginia [UVA] climatologist Patrick Michaels found that, in the Atlantic basin, the hurricane formation area with the best data over the longest period, the "trend" observed by the Webster team disappears once data going back to 1940 are included. . . .

Very Gradual Increases in Storm Strength

Hurricanes are heat engines, so it is likely that global warming will increase the number, strength, or formation area of hurricanes—or a combination of these—*to some extent*. But by how much is unclear. Thomas Knutson of NOAA and Robert Tuleya of Old Dominion University estimated in a 2004 study that a 2.0°C rise in maximum SSTs would increase hurricane wind speed by about 6 percent over 80 years. Comments UVA's Michaels, "That means global warming is likely to be responsible, right now, for at best, an increase of about 0.6 percent in hurricane wind speeds—raising a decent hurricane of 120 mph to 120.7 mph, a change too small to measure."

Knutson and Tuleya came to pretty much the same conclusion: "From our standpoint, the small 0.9 degree Fahrenheit [or about 0.4°C] warming observed in the Atlantic since 1900 implies only a 2–3 miles per hour intensity increase to date. Such a small increase is hard to detect. It is difficult to attribute the upswing in strong hurricane activity this past season to global warming. Season-to-season variability is very large."

Inconsistent Cyclone Strength

The Atlantic is not the only region to suffer hurricane-strength storms. Alarmists often claim that Japan has seen an increase in typhoon activity due to global warming. Figure 2 shows the number of tropical storms and typhoon (Tropical Cyclone) over the Western North Pacific [WNP], from 1950 through 2005. The data simply do not reveal a linear trend corresponding to the gradual increase in atmospheric CO_2 levels. Further, whether a particular storm "hits" Japan—its trajectory—depends on local meteorological factors, not on average global temperatures.

> *Alarmists are using scare tactics and overstatements of the science to promote specific policies, most prominently a worldwide reduction in fossil fuel use.*

Australia, meanwhile, suffers from cyclones. Alarmists point to Cyclone Monica of April 2006, which was stronger than both Katrina and Rita, as proof that global warming is making storms stronger everywhere. Monica attained wind speeds of 180 mph, making it the strongest cyclone of 2006. But it was neither the strongest cyclone ever measured or an indication that storms are getting stronger. At least five U.S. hurricanes had equal or greater wind speeds, including Hurricane Doug, attaining a wind speed of 185 mph on September 6, 1950, and Hurricane Camille, attaining a wind speed of 190 mph on August 17, 1969. More importantly, Australia's hurricane season in 2006 was not exceptional. According to NOAA:

"The tropical cyclone season in the Australian region has been near average with the development of 12 storms, two more than average. Although final assessments of tropical cyclone strength are continuing, it is thought that 25 percent of these storms reached Category 5 strength on the Australian scale.". . .

America Needs to Focus on Preparedness

Alarmists are using scare tactics and overstatements of the science to promote specific policies, most prominently a world-wide reduction in fossil fuel use to reduce the greenhouse gas emissions that contribute to some extent to a warming atmosphere. The Kyoto Protocol, which the United States has rejected, is the flagship for such policies. However, since Kyoto would avert an immeasurably small amount of global warming by 2050 (0.07°C), Kyoto-style approaches can provide *no protection* from hurricanes in the policy-relevant future. It is disingenuous for activists to claim that a hurricane-warming link justifies changes in U.S. energy policy. Indeed, hyping such a link can be counterproductive—if people seek protection from hurricanes via climate change policy, they are apt to neglect the practical preparedness measures that can actually save lives.

The alarmists' position begs the question of whether, if greenhouse gas reduction policies had been put in place 20 years ago, Hurricane Katrina would not have happened or nearly as destructive. Yet no reputable scientist has yet stated that Katrina happened because of global warming. This underscores the simple truth that hurricanes, including very damaging ones, will happen whether or not greenhouse gas reduction policies are put in place. . . .

United States hurricane policy must not be dictated by global warming concerns. Diverting resources that would otherwise be spent on protecting vulnerable communities into climate change policies would unnecessarily increase those communities' hurricane vulnerability. In preparing for hurricanes, global warming policies constitute both a red herring and a white elephant.

9

Carbon Dioxide Emissions Must Be Rationed to Reduce Global Warming

Mark Lynas

A freelance journalist focusing on climate change, Mark Lynas has written articles for the Guardian, Observer, Independent, *and other British publications. He is also the author of* High Tide: News from a Warming World.

If the world is serious about countering global warming, humanity will have to drastically reduce carbon dioxide (CO_2) emissions. To do this, countries will have to submit to carbon rationing. That is, all nations will be given an allotment of CO_2 emissions that they can produce. If one nation does not need to meet its quota of production shares, it may sell or trade them to other countries that overproduce emissions. This plan must trickle down to individual households as well, so that families are given rations of emissions that they can buy, sell, or trade. Only by uniting in this common cause can the globe truly contain the amount of carbon dioxide emissions that otherwise would contribute to planetary overheating.

The best indication of whether a person truly grasps the scale of the global climate crisis is not whether they drive a hybrid car or offset their flights, nor whether they subscribe to the *Ecologist* or plan to attach a wind turbine to their house. The most reliable indicator is whether they support carbon

Mark Lynas, "Why We Must Ration the Future," *New Statesman*, October 23, 2006, pp. 12–14. Copyright © 2006 *New Statesman*, Ltd. Reproduced by permission.

rationing. The received political wisdom is that the general public will recoil in horror at a scheme whose very name recalls wartime national emergencies and austerity. Rationing is the opposite of today's consumerist free-for-all, where economic growth is the highest of government policy.

But that is precisely the point. It is because carbon rationing represents a total break with business as usual that it is the only climate-change policy that will work. Let me put it simply: if we go on emitting greenhouse gases at anything like the current rate, most of the surface of the globe will be rendered uninhabitable within the lifetimes of most readers of this article. We must reduce our emissions by 90 per cent or so within three or four decades if we are to have any chance of avoiding this looming catastrophe.

That challenge requires collective, conscious action, involving a planned transition from a high-carbon economy to a low-carbon one. Just as we did not hope to win the Second World War by muddling through with a pre-1939 economy, we cannot hope to face down today's emergency without completely altering our national priorities. Defeating [Adolf] Hitler was our number-one aim in 1940: it ranked above health, education, crime and all the other day-to-day concerns of government, requiring a supreme effort of mobilisation. Defeating global warming must be our priority today, or we will lose this war, and with it our very existence as a civilisation.

Rationing Is Inevitable, Equity Is Inevitable

At an international level, some variant of rationing is nothing less than a mathematical inevitability. Let us assume that at some stage in the near future—perhaps after a change of regime in Washington, DC—world governments hammer out an agreement about what constitutes a "dangerous" level of carbon dioxide in the atmosphere. Today, atmospheric CO_2 stands at 380 parts per million by volume (ppm), a higher level than at any time since the Eocene era (35 to 55 million years ago). According to the modellers, stabilising at 400ppm yields a three-to-one chance that global temperature increases would level off on this side of 2°C, saving us from calamitous rates of sea-level rise and a mass extinction that would otherwise wipe out more than half of life on earth.

But this 400ppm target means that only 80 billion tonnes more carbon can be emitted by humanity over the next few decades. This figure is non-negotiable: you can't bargain with the atmosphere. How the remaining carbon budget is divided between human beings, however, involves a decision about rationing. The most likely outcome is that it will be divided among the world's countries on the basis of their populations—in other words, we will all get an equal ration.

If climate change is to be solved, global emissions will have to contract (to sustainable levels) and converge (towards zero).

Equity is inevitable, and not because future world leaders will be bleeding-heart liberals, but because no developing-world government will ever accede to an agreement that freezes existing global inequalities. The choice of facing rich-country governments, in other words, is between inequity or survival. The government of India, for example, will not sign an agreement that gives its people 20 times less of the remaining budget on a per-person basis than Americans get, and nor should it be expected to. China will not sign a document that gives the Chinese only a third of what British people receive. (Annual per-capita carbon-dioxide emissions are approximately one tonne in India, 20 tonnes in the United States, ten tonnes in the UK [United Kingdom] and three tonnes in China.) Indeed, given the rich world's disproportionate historical responsibility for causing climate change, developing countries may well demand a higher ration of the remaining budget than rich countries receive.

Contraction and Convergence

This mathematical equation, of a convergence towards equal per-capita carbon allocations in the context of a contraction of overall global emissions, is the framework known as contraction and convergence (C&C). Many people—environmentalists included—have railed against it, but no one has ever been able to propose a viable alternative. Plenty of other initiatives and proposals exist (of which the Kyoto Protocol is one) but they all add up to nothing more than guesswork, with no definable outcome, when set against the remorseless logical framework of C&C.

If climate change is to be solved, global emissions will have to contract (to sustainable levels) and converge (towards zero). There is no other way to join the dots on the graph. The question is whether world leaders will face the inevitable before it is too late. If we are to hit the 400ppm target, scarcely a decade remains before we must begin cutting emissions across the whole global economy. And after that particular climatic window closes, global warming may spiral quickly out of control.

To say that 400ppm is an ambitious target is a colossal understatement: Sir David King has advocated 550ppm as the lowest politically achievable target. Given his role as chief scientific adviser to the [British] government. Sir David is presumably aware that this represents nothing less than a death sentence for half the world's population. In advocating it, he is veering dangerously close to what some campaigners have called "the economics of genocide". It is irrelevant to the biosphere what any of us considers to be "politically realistic": it obeys the hard laws of physics and chemistry, not the rather more flexible laws of economics and politics.

Make Carbon Allocations Tradeable

Domestic carbon rationing is the national corollary of contraction and convergence. Like the monetary budget within which all governments and individuals are accustomed to operating, the carbon budget is non-negotiable. Unlike "green taxes" or any of the other assorted climate policies recently discussed at party conferences, only a top-down carbon rationing scheme can deliver a predetermined outcome with any certainty. Whether taxes, for instance, actually reduce carbon consumption depends on what people are prepared to pay. Taxes are also important to raise revenue, presenting the government with a conflict of interest.

Trading [emissions rations] gives a financial incentive for low-carbon innovations.

Moreover, taxation is simply a hidden way of rationing via the price mechanism—something likely to be as unpopular as it is unfair. If conspicuous carbon consumption by the rich goes unchallenged. . . any popular effort on climate change will collapse, just as the war effort would have been fatally undermined had the royal family been given a higher food ration in 1940. Instead, the sight of aristocrats and dock workers all mucking in showed a country united in its determination to defeat Nazism.

One important difference from wartime rationing is that future carbon allocations would need to be tradeable in order to make the system flexible. If person A really wants to fly to Australia to see his mother, and person B (who doesn't have a car) is happy to sell him some unused quota, so much the better—the overall objective of carbon reduction is still achieved (because the annual national budget declines), but people don't lose their freedom of action. Moreover, trading gives a financial incentive for low-carbon innovations: if a new invention needs less of your ration, it will become more attractive. If having solar panels on your house allows you to cash in your unused ration, they become not just affordable, but desirable. At a macro level, business has an incentive to make long-term investment decisions.

For individuals, carbon rationing would operate as a parallel currency: when purchasing high-carbon goods (petrol for a car, overseas flights) a proportion of carbon currency would be surrendered at the point of sale. Given that only half the national carbon output stems from individuals' direct choices, the other half would probably be auctioned by the government to private business to cover manufacturing and services. So if you're buying bananas or having a haircut, the carbon ration will already have been paid for by the company, and its cost built into the end price for the consumer.

A System Ready for the Public Embraced

Unlike the ration books of the wartime era, modern rationing could be electronic, operating on the same principle as debit cards do with a current account. If a person lacks the carbon credits to cover a purchase, he or she could buy on the "spot" market at the point of sale, just as pay-as-you-go mobile-phone users top up their credit in order to make a call.

So will the general public accept rationing? David Miliband, the [British] Environment Secretary, one of the few senior politicians who seems to "get it" on climate change, suggests they will, and floated the idea of carbon rationing at a major speech to the Audit Commission on 19 July. I am told privately that, for the Conservatives, Oliver Letwin is an "anorak" on the issue, having spent hours poring over the nuts and bolts of a rationing scheme. Most surprisingly, whenever I propose carbon rationing at public meetings around the country, it seems to generate a spontaneous round of applause. Perhaps the public is less backward on climate change than many politicians like to assume. Perhaps people also realise that the kind of society carbon rationing would usher in, with resurgent communities and small-scale agriculture, would actually be highly beneficial for most of us.

Nevertheless, imposing such a scheme—and imposed it must be, as participation could not be voluntary—would require political leadership and vision of the sort that seems to be in scarce supply in today's corridors of power. But such leadership need not, in the long term, be unpopular. Nor would it be incompatible with democracy. Who would march in [London's] Trafalgar Square against solving climate change? Probably about as many people as marched against rationing in 1940: none.

10

Carbon Dioxide Emissions Are Not the Cause of Global Warming

Robert J. Cihak

Robert J. Cihak is a senior fellow and board member of the Discovery Institute, an organization that promotes public policy based on the traditions of representative government, the free market, and individual liberty. A medical doctor, Cihak is also a former president of the Association of American Physicians and Surgeons.

Carbon dioxide (CO_2) has always been a part of the earth's atmosphere, and the planet's current warming trend is generating more CO_2. This accumulation has natural causes linked to the sun and the earth's orbit; it has nothing to do with human production of relatively miniscule amounts of CO_2. Most informed observers, in fact, fear that the warming trend will end, and the planet will suffer another ice age. Until then, a little warming is not likely to adversely affect humanity.

All the recent worry about carbon dioxide (CO_2) in the air is even more out of proportion than the now-dissipating worries about [the pesticide] DDT for malaria control. . . .

DDT alarmists caused tens of millions of unnecessary deaths, plus billions of cases of unnecessary malarial illnesses and debilitating effects.

Let's not allow CO_2 hysteria to kill millions more.

In contrast with human-created DDT, CO_2 a "greenhouse gas" has been part of the earth's atmosphere as long as the earth has existed. About 450 million years ago, the earth's atmospheric CO_2 level was about 2,000 percent higher than it is today, at the same time the earth's atmosphere was about the same temperature as today.

In trying to control the atmosphere's CO_2 levels, such as under the Kyoto Protocol Treaty, alarmists would likely inflict a human death toll comparable to the malaria epidemic, if the professional and amateur CO_2 worriers have their way. Trying to control CO_2 levels would be much more harmful to human health than any possible benefit.

Human creativity and adaptability have largely overcome the ever-present vagaries of weather and climate change.

New Views on CO_2

In a new book, *Unstoppable Global Warming: Every 1,500 Years* (Rowman & Littlefield, 2007), S. Fred Singer and Dennis T. Avery report recent scientific discoveries about the earth's climate. Dr. Singer is a Ph.D. climate physicist, founding dean of the School of Environmental and Planetary Science at the University of Miami, and first director of the U.S. National Weather Satellite Service. Avery is a senior fellow of the Hudson Institute, a former senior analyst in the U.S. Department of State, and an expert on agriculture and the environment policy.

The authors alternate chapters evaluating scientific evidence and political manipulations with six "baseless fear" chapters addressing false tales about changes in sea level, species extinction, drought, storms, global cooling, and human deaths.

One of the new and fascinating observations is that CO_2 changes follow rather than precede climate fluctuations. As Dr. Singer puts it, "CO_2 changes have lagged about 800 years behind the temperature changes. Global warming has produced more CO_2, rather than more CO_2 producing global warming." CO_2 is innocent.

This turns the entire basis for the Kyoto Treaty on its head. These scientific advances show that CO_2 worriers are like people who confuse cause and effect. This is sort of like saying fallen-down trees bring on high winds and storms; most of us recognize that storms can bring high winds and that the high winds blow trees over, not the other way around.

For about two decades in each period, the earth warmed a bit, starting in about 1850 and 1920, the total temperature change was about 0.8 degrees Celsius. Some cooling spells also intervened.

The High Cost and Limited Value of Kyoto

Since 1850, the productivity, general wealth and living standards of the human race improved substantially, despite wars and massive human sacrifices at the hands of communists, Nazis and other oppressive tyrants. Human creativity and adaptability have largely overcome the ever-present vagaries of weather and climate change.

Environmentalist Bjorn Lomborg, in his book *The Skeptical Environmentalist*, estimated that implementing the Kyoto Treaty would cost at least $150 billion every year. UNICEF [United Nations International Children's Emergency Fund] estimates that "$80 billion per year could give all Third World inhabitants access to the basics like health, education, water, and sanitation."

As Dr. Singer says "Science is the process of developing theories and testing them against observations until they are proven true or false." Science is a search for truth based on evidence, not a search for consensus of beliefs.

Canadian geologist Jan Veizer notes, "Models and empirical observation are both indispensable tools of science, yet when discrepancies arise, observations should carry greater weight than theory." In other words, pay more attention to the evidence you can see than to what scientists make up, even if they're showing you computer printouts.

The computer climate models did not predict some recent climate-influencing phenomena. For example, based on satellite weather measurements, NASA [National Aeronautics and Space Administration] researchers found an unpredicted massive loss of heat over the tropical Pacific Ocean.

This "heat vent emitted about as much energy during the 1980s and 1990s as would have been generated by an instant doubling of the air's CO_2 content" according to Dr. Singer.

In addition to not predicting this event, climate scientists have not been able to fit their computer models to these unpredicted observations. Based on this and other failures, Dr. Singer concludes, "We can't trust the climate models at all."

Even global warming tree believers admit that the Kyoto Treaty would have, at best, a miniscule and undetectable effect of less than 0.05 degrees Celsius on global temperature.

The Role of the Sun and the Earth's Orbit

Yes, global warming, global cooling, and greenhouse gases are real and natural phenomena. But scientific evidence points to activity in the sun, plus changes in the earth's orbit and the earth's axis, as much more significant factors underlying global climate change.

Several different solar cycles overlap and reinforce each other about every 1,500 years, in addition to multiple other cycles. Worldwide climates changed up to several degrees Celsius over each of these 1,500-year cycles.

Over the last million years, each major climate cycle has lasted about 100,000 years. Ice ages lasting about 90,000 years have alternated with 10,000 years long "interglacial warm periods." Our current interglacial warmth started about 12,000 years ago.

Temperatures during the ice ages were 7 degrees to 12 degrees Celsius lower than today, a much wider swing lasting much longer than the 1,500-year cycle.

As Dr. Singer says, "The climate event that deserves real concern is the next big ice age. That is inevitably approaching, though it may, still be thousands of years away. When it comes, temperatures may plummet 15 degrees Celsius, with the high latitudes getting up to 40 degrees colder."

So why does the CO_2 controversy continue? Perhaps French President Jacques Chirac gave the game away in 2000 when he said that the Kyoto Protocol Treaty represents "the first component of an authentic global governance."

We suspect that many politicians and others are jumping on this bandwagon to enhance their personal power, prestige, and pay.

Call it the global-political-industrial-media, complex, if you want.

Healthy Planet, Prosperous Planet

So, what is best for the health and well-being of humanity? Not only is global warming not a threat, it's likely to be a boon to mankind, as it was in the 900 A.D. to 1300 A.D. medieval warming and in the 200 B.C. to 600 A.D. Roman warming. Current political moves internationally, nationally and even in the city of Seattle [Washington] and other localities to control CO_2 only benefit those few on the payroll or on power trips.

The rest of us are made poorer and less healthy.

People are smart. They move out of the way of growing glaciers. If they live on sinking land threatened by storm floods, at least some move to higher ground (unless they're making good money off flood insurance). Most people retire to warmer, not colder, climates.

People's health and lives are better, longer, more productive, and more fun in wealthy societies than in poor ones.

Wealthy is healthy.

We've always had hot and cold climate spells. In recent centuries, human progress has outpaced changes due to weather and climate.

Whether she blows hot or cold, it's more effective and wiser to use resources to adapt to the Mother Nature's whims than to try to change her ways.

11

The United States Should Ratify the Kyoto Protocol

Citizens for Global Solutions

Citizens for Global Solutions is an advocacy organization that informs the American public on a variety of issues that threaten global peace and well-being. The organization also seeks to aid policy makers in addressing the nation's response to these global issues, stressing the value of worldwide cooperative action.

Drafted in 1997 and taking effect in February 2005, the Kyoto Protocol is an international agreement calling on signatory nations to successively cut greenhouse gas emissions over a series of target dates. The United States signed on the treaty under the Bill Clinton administration but neither Clinton nor his successor, George W. Bush, sent the treaty to Congress to be ratified. In order for the nation to show its commitment to stop global warming, the United States should join the world consensus and ratify the Kyoto Protocol.

Climate change is one of the most serious challenges the world faces today. Its effects are not limited to one nation or particular region of the globe; rather, they will affect humanity and ecosystems worldwide. Concentrations of atmospheric greenhouse gases, believed to trap heat in the atmosphere in a planetary "greenhouse" of sorts, have risen sharply, as have global temperatures. Scientists predict that the average world temperature will rise enough this century to significantly affect both aquatic and terrestrial ecosystems. Sea levels along the coasts of the United States could rise by as much as 2 feet, which would certainly cause mass displacement in coastal areas. Agricultural output may decrease because of varied growing seasons, unpredictable precipitation patterns, and quicker evaporation, which reduces soil moisture necessary for growth. Finally, extreme weather events, like hurricanes and severe droughts, are likely to become much more common and severe.

What is the source of these rising temperatures? Scientists and historians say that clear-cutting forests, irresponsible farming methods, poor waste management, and, most of all, the burning of coal, oil, gas, and other carbon-based fuels have substantially increased the concentration of greenhouse gases in the Earth's atmosphere.

Fortunately, through global partnership, there is much we can do to stop or even reverse these disconcerting trends. The international community has embraced the Kyoto Protocol, which went into effect on February 16, 2005, as an important first step in protecting our children and grandchildren from the undesirable effects of major climate change. The United States, however, in a departure from its tradition of global leadership, did not ratify the Protocol.

Kyoto Facts

The Kyoto Protocol was negotiated within the United Nations Framework Convention on Climate Change (UNFCCC) as part of a larger UN effort to promote sustainable development around the globe. The treaty was negotiated in Kyoto, Japan in 1997 and opened for signature in March of 1998. By the date on which it took effect in February of 2005, over 140 nations had ratified the treaty, including Russia, a major emitter of carbon dioxide and other greenhouse gases. Only two countries that had initially signed the treaty did not ratify: the United States and Australia.

The Treaty sets a number of environmental goals, the most significant of which are targets for greenhouse gas emissions reductions. Under the Kyoto Protocol, industrialized countries agree to reduce their emissions of six greenhouse gases to an average of 5.2% below 1990 levels by 2012.

Emissions Trading

To reach these targets, the participating countries agreed to set up a program for emissions trading. Emissions trading is considered one of the most, if not the most, cost-effective manners of reducing any type of contaminant emission, be it a greenhouse gas, air pollutant, or water pollutant. Under the Kyoto Protocol, greenhouse gas emissions are categorized into "units" (of usually one ton each) and treated as entities to be bought, sold, and stored in a global greenhouse gas market.

The scheme allows each country to choose how to most cost-effectively reduce its emissions. The "soft cap" of 5.2% below 1990 levels of greenhouse gas emissions makes the program work: a country may not exceed its emissions limit unless it purchases extra units from another country that does not use all of its credits. That gives other countries an incentive to reduce their pollution well below their assigned caps, so that they can have credits to sell.

The U.S. emits more greenhouse gases than any other country—nearly a quarter of the world's total—even though it represents only 4% of the world's population.

Here are examples of two countries with different financial scenarios. Let's say that Country A can reduce greenhouse gas emissions relatively cheaply. For Country A, it makes the most economic sense to purchase and install machinery that will reduce its emissions beyond its required levels and sell its extra credits to another country. Country B, however, may find these purchases and installation more expensive than purchasing surplus credits from another country. It may make the most sense, financially, for this country to exceed its allotted emissions levels and purchase emissions credits from another country that has not used all of its credits. All of this must be done without exceeding the cap for total emissions levels.

The Clean Development Mechanism, "Bubbling," and Sinks

The Kyoto Protocol also allows for industrialized countries to earn additional emissions credits by helping to reduce greenhouse gas emissions in developing countries. This method of gaining credits and minimizing climate change under an emissions trading scheme has been named the Clean Development Mechanism. The Mechanism is designed to help less-developed-countries contribute to the mission of the Treaty, while providing incentives to industrialized countries to facilitate such projects.

In addition, any group of developed countries may create a "bubble" to meet the total emissions requirements of the group. Using such an approach, countries are allowed to redistribute emissions credits as long as the total of their levels is preserved. "Bubbling" was designed for smaller countries, many of which are in Europe, that already rely on each other for assistance and trade.

Finally, the Kyoto Protocol assigns value to carbon sinks, places that extract and absorb carbon from the atmosphere. Forests, soil, and oceans are all major carbon sinks. Kyoto allows member nations with large areas of forest (or other vegetation) to deduct the estimated value of the forest-stored carbon from their assigned emissions levels. By giving them an incentive to preserve these forests as sinks, the Protocol gives countries with sinks more flexibility with which to achieve their targets.

The United States Needs to Join World Consensus

The United States signed onto the Treaty under the [Bill] Clinton administration, but the [George W.] Bush Administration has refused to submit it to the Senate for ratification. The U.S. emits more greenhouse gases than any other country—nearly a quarter of the world's total—even though it represents only 4% of the world's population. While other industrialized nations are taking action, the Bush Administration continues to ignore the scientific consensus that human activity is causing changes in the global climate that will have serious impacts on people's lives for years to come.

The Kyoto Treaty is the first step in a global effort to address climate change seriously. The United States, traditionally at the forefront of innovation and bold action, needs to join its peers in protecting the world against the risk of climate change.

12

The United States Was Right to Reject the Kyoto Protocol

Nick Schulz

Nick Schulz owns and runs TechCentralStation, a pro-capitalist Web site, and is the editor of the site's TCS Daily *news organ.*

The Kyoto Protocol—an international treaty to limit greenhouse gas emissions—is impractical because it sets unrealistic targets, and the cost of trying to reach those targets would be prohibitively expensive. In addition, the framework of the treaty is unfair because it allows developing nations to produce more emissions than developed countries, thus skewing global economics in favor of newly industrializing competitors such as China and India. The United States government has so far been correct in refusing to ratify the agreement in its current form.

Buenos Aires—"No to Bush, Yes to Kyoto" reads a slogan adorning the credentialing lanyards draped around the necks of several delegates and journalists here at the United Nations' tenth annual climate-change conference (COP 10) [which met in 2004]. But the U.S. president [George W. Bush] is an odd choice for a villain. A more accurate reflection of what's happening on the ground would be the slogan, "Yes to Bush, No to Kyoto."

The Kyoto Protocol—the global treaty drafted to reduce emissions of greenhouse gases in order to prevent global warming—is set to go into effect [in 2005, which it did]. It will do so, much to the chagrin of many European bureau-

Nick Schulz, "Fatally Flawed," *National Review Online*, December 15, 2004. Reproduced by permission.

crats and green activists, without the participation of the United States. Early in his first term, President Bush labeled the treaty "fatally flawed" and announced the U.S. would not participate in its schedule of forced emissions reductions.

Why Kyoto Was Rejected

President Bush rejected Kyoto for a few simple reasons. First, it would impose significant economic damage on the American economy (a [Bill] Clinton administration report on the costs of Kyoto put the tab at $300 billion per year). Second, the reduction targets and timetables were impractical from a technological perspective. Third, the treaty exempted developing economies such as India and China from any restrictions even though their emissions are rising rapidly. Instead, the Bush team under Secretary of Energy Spencer Abraham charted a different course, which involved investment in basic research, technology transfer to poor countries, and bilateral agreements.

Critics cried foul at President Bush's "unilateral" decision and questioned his motives, saying he was ignoring scientific evidence and rewarding fossil-fuel producers and users who supported him politically. It's too bad the critics focused on the administration's alleged motives and not its arguments. As it turns out, several key players in the climate-change debate are starting to come around to President Bush's view.

Developing Nations Already Backing Out

On the first day of the conference, a group of developing countries, including China, announced that they would not commit to any specific emissions reductions in the future. Gao Feng, a top official in the Chinese foreign ministry, boldly stated: "We are a developing country, we're not yet making international commitments. . . . We will continue to attend to our energy needs. We will need to increase our energy consumption for the next 30 to 50 years."

In an important forthcoming book on energy trends, *The Bottomless Well*, Peter Huber of the Manhattan Institute and Mark Mills, a former consultant to the White House Science Office under President [Ronald] Reagan, explain developing country demand. "How . . . can anyone responsibly favor the burning of more hydrocarbons?" they ask. "The short answer is that, for most people, the only practical alternative today is to burn carbohydrates [wood, biomass], and that's much worse."

[Climate-concerned] organizations . . . are beginning to focus more on adaptation—as opposed to mitigation—in part because the emissions reductions called for in Kyoto are too costly and technologically infeasible.

The developing nations have been bolstered by an uncomfortable fact for Kyoto supporters. Several Kyoto participants, including most European nations, will not meet their stated emissions-reduction targets. Data from the Paris-based International Energy Agency (IEA) forecasts that European emissions will grow rapidly, increasing by as much as 25 percent by 2030. Several Kyoto signatories in Europe are already 20 to 30 percent above their emissions targets. If the Europeans can't drastically reduce their emissions, developing-country representatives reasoned, they have little reason to make similar pledges.

Focus on Weathering Climate Change

Then on Monday [December 13, 2004], the Pew Center on Global Climate Change, a key Kyoto cheerleader and a player in climate-change negotiations for years, issued a new report, "Climate Data: Insights and Observations." A co-author of the report, Jonathan Pershing of the World Resources Institute, said, "We are beginning to see more research on adaptation strategies in response to climate change." Adaptation means having the capacity to handle climate changes of any kind, and organizations like Pew are beginning to focus more on adaptation—as opposed to mitigation—in part because the emissions reductions called for in Kyoto are too costly and technologically infeasible.

This is a sensible move by Pew. The focus on adaptation to climate change—whether that change is human influenced or not—will be a boon to poor countries around the world. These countries are most vulnerable to climate changes because they lack the wealth and infrastructure to handle hazardous events such as heat waves, cold spells, hurricanes, and floods. A new appreciation for boosting developing-country adaptive capacity, and a new respect for the tools that make it possible—such as free trade, property rights, and the rule of law—are welcome developments.

Lastly, at a forum on Tuesday [December 14], Italian environment minister Corrado Clini admitted to Kyoto's huge structural flaws and its current inability to deal adequately with the challenges posed by climate changes. Acknowledging the growing global need for secure energy resources, particularly by poor countries hoping to raise their living standards, Clini argued that "a much broader long-term strategy, and much more global effective measures, than those within the Kyoto Protocol, are needed, involving both developed and emerging economies."

In other words, the Kyoto Protocol is "fatally flawed."

13

America Could Stop Global Warming if It Wanted To

Gregg Easterbrook

A fellow at the Brookings Institution, Gregg Easterbrook is a contributing editor of the Atlantic Monthly, *the* New Republic, *and the* Washington Monthly.

Global warming is nearly always debated in pessimistic tones, implying that only drastic changes can halt catastrophe or that solutions adopted in the United States will be very expensive and insignificant given the pollutants coming from large developing nations such as China and India. However, as in the past, fixes to air pollution problems in the United States have usually been easy and cheap, and there is no reason to suppose that greenhouse gas emissions cannot be similarly addressed. And if American ingenuity can rise to the problem, the resulting solutions can be easily passed on to other nations to reverse the global warming trend. Americans should look at this problem optimistically, acknowledging that with effort global warming can be halted to avert crisis.

If there is now a scientific consensus that global warming must be taken seriously, there is also a related political consensus: that the issue is Gloom City. In [the movie and the book] *An Inconvenient Truth*, [former vice president] Al Gore warns of sea levels rising to engulf New York and San Francisco and implies that only wrenching lifestyle sacrifice can save us. The opposing view is just as glum. Even mild restrictions on greenhouse gases could "cripple our economy," Republican Senator Kit Bond of Missouri said in 2003. Other conservatives suggest that greenhouse-gas rules for Americans would be pointless anyway, owing to increased fossil-fuel use in China and India. When commentators hash this issue out it's often a contest to see which side can sound more pessimistic.

Just Another Air-Pollution Problem

Here's a different way of thinking about the greenhouse effect: that action to prevent runaway global warming may prove cheap, practical, effective, and totally consistent with economic growth. Which makes a body wonder: Why is such environmental optimism absent from American political debate?

Greenhouse gases are an air-pollution problem—and all previous air-pollution problems have been reduced faster and more cheaply than predicted, without economic harm. Some of these problems once seemed scary and intractable, just as greenhouse gases seem today. About forty years ago urban smog was increasing so fast that President Lyndon Johnson warned, "Either we stop poisoning our air or we become a nation [in] gas masks groping our way through dying cities." During Ronald Reagan's presidency, emissions of chlorofluorocarbons, or CFCs, threatened to deplete the stratospheric ozone layer. As recently as George H. W. Bush's administration, acid rain was said to threaten a "new silent spring" of dead Appalachian forests.

But in each case, strong regulations were enacted, and what happened? Since 1970, smog-forming air pollution has declined by a third to a half. Emissions of CFCs have been nearly eliminated, and studies suggest that ozone-layer replenishment is beginning. Acid rain, meanwhile, has declined by a third since 1990, while Appalachian forest health has improved sharply.

Cheap Fixes

Most progress against air pollution has been cheaper than expected. Smog controls on automobiles, for example, were predicted to cost thousands of dollars for each vehicle. Today's new cars emit less than 2 percent as much smog-forming pollution as the cars of 1970, and the cars are still as affordable today as they were then. Acid-rain control has cost about 10 percent of what was predicted in 1990, when Congress enacted new rules. At that time, opponents said the regulations would cause a "clean-air recession;" instead, the economy boomed.

Polls show that Americans think the air is getting dirtier, not cleaner, perhaps because media coverage of the environment rarely if ever mentions improvements.

Greenhouse gases, being global, are the biggest air-pollution problem ever faced. And because widespread fossil-fuel use is inevitable for some time to come, the best-case scenario for the next few decades may be a slowing of the rate of greenhouse-gas buildup, to prevent runaway climate change. Still, the basic pattern observed in all other forms of air-pollution control—rapid progress at low cost—should repeat for greenhouse-gas controls.

Yet a paralyzing negativism dominates global-warming politics. Environmentalists depict climate change as nearly unstoppable; skeptics speak of the problem as either imaginary (the "greatest hoax ever perpetrated," in the words of Senator James Inhofe, chairman of the Senate's environment committee) or ruinously expensive to address.

Even conscientious politicians may struggle for views that aren't dismal. Mandy Grunwald, a Democratic political consultant, says, "when political candidates talk about new energy sources, they use a positive, can-do vocabulary. Voters have personal experience with energy use, so they can relate to discussion of solutions. If you say a car can use a new kind of fuel, this makes intuitive sense to people. But global warming is of such scale and magnitude, people don't have any commonsense way to grasp what the solutions would be. So political candidates tend to talk about the greenhouse effect in a depressing way."

Hidden Environmental Accomplishments

One reason the global-warming problem seems so daunting is that the success of previous anti-pollution efforts remains something of a secret. Polls show that Americans think the air is getting dirtier, not cleaner, perhaps because media coverage of the environment rarely if ever mentions improvements. For instance, did you know that smog and acid rain have continued to diminish throughout George W. Bush's presidency?

Making the [global warming] problem appear unsolvable encourages a sort of listless fatalism, blunting the drive to take first steps toward a solution.

One might expect Democrats to trumpet the decline of air pollution, which stands as one of government's leading postwar achievements. But just as Republicans have found they can bash Democrats by falsely accusing them of being soft on defense, Democrats have found they can bash Republicans by falsely accusing them of destroying the environment. If that's your argument, you might skip over the evidence that many environmental trends are positive. One might also expect Republicans to trumpet the reduction of air pollution, since it signifies responsible behavior by industry. But to acknowledge that air pollution has declined would require Republicans to say the words, "The regulations worked."

Does it matter that so many in politics seem so pessimistic about the prospect of addressing global warming? Absolutely. Making the problem appear unsolvable encourages a sort of listless fatalism, blunting the drive to take first steps toward a solution. Historically, first steps against air pollution have often led to pleasant surprises. When Congress, in 1970, mandated major reductions in smog caused by automobiles, even many supporters of the rule feared it would be hugely expensive. But the catalytic converter was not practical then; soon it was perfected, and suddenly, major reductions in smog became affordable. Even a small step by the United States against greenhouse gases could lead to a similar breakthrough.

Technological Solutions Can Spread Across the Globe

And to those who worry that any greenhouse-gas reductions in the United States will be swamped by new emissions from China and India, here's a final reason to be optimistic: technology can move across borders with considerable speed. Today it's not clear that American inventors or entrepreneurs can make money by reducing greenhouse gases, so relatively few are trying. But suppose the United States regulated greenhouse gases, using its own domestic program, not the cumbersome Kyoto Protocol [an international agreement to limit carbon dioxide emissions]; then America's formidable entrepreneurial and engineering communities would fully engage the problem. Innovations pioneered here could spread throughout the world, and suddenly rapid global warming would not seem inevitable.

The two big technical advances against smog—the catalytic converter and the chemical engineering that removes pollutants from gasoline at the refinery stage—were invented in the United States. The big economic advance against acid rain—a credit-trading system that gives power-plant managers a profit incentive to reduce pollution—was pioneered here as well. These advances are now spreading globally. Smog and acid rain are still increasing in some parts of the world, but the trend lines suggest that both will decline fairly soon, even in developing nations. For instance, two decades ago urban smog was rising at a dangerous rate in Mexico; today it is diminishing there, though the country's population continues to grow. A short time ago declining smog and acid rain in developing nations seemed an impossibility; today declining greenhouse gases seem an impossibility. The history of air-pollution control says otherwise.

Americans love challenges, and preventing artificial climate change is just the sort of technological and economic challenge at which this nation excels. It only remains for the right politician to recast the challenge in practical, optimistic tones. Gore seldom has, and Bush seems to have no interest in trying. But cheap and fast improvement is not a pipe dream; it is the pattern of previous efforts against air pollution. The only reason runaway global warming seems unstoppable is that we have not yet tried to stop it.

Organizations to Contact

The editors have compiled the following list of organizations concerned with the issues debated in this book. The descriptions are derived from materials provided by the organizations. All have publications or information available for interested readers. The list was compiled on the date of publication of the present volume; the information provided here may change. Be aware that many organizations take several weeks or longer to respond to inquiries, so allow as much time as possible.

Council on Foreign Relations (CFR)
58 E. 68th St., New York, NY   10021
(212) 434-9400 • fax: (212) 434-9800
e-mail: communications@cfr.org
Web site: www.cfr.org

The Council on Foreign Relations is a nonpartisan organization seeking to promote understanding of America's role in the world through its foreign policy. The council convenes forums on important issues, operates a think tank where prominent international affairs scholars can conduct research and write, commissions books and reports, such as "Why We Should Plan to Pay for Nation-Building," and publishes *Foreign Affairs*, a journal of global politics.

Education for Peace in Iraq Center (EPIC)
1101 Pennsylvania Ave. SE, Washington, DC   20003
(202) 543-6176
Web site: www.epic-usa.org

The Education for Peace in Iraq Center is a nonprofit organization that seeks to promote policies and programs that benefit and support Iraqi citizens. The EPIC blog is updated daily to provide information from a wide variety of news sources, journals, and research publications. EPIC *Dispatches* is an online publication providing Iraq analysis, field reports, and links to Iraqi sources. EPIC's *Iraq Forum* is a series of policy seminars on the Iraq situation. Audio transcripts are available on EPIC's Web site, including discussions such as "Iraqi Views on the Aftermath of War and Post-Conflict Reconstruction."

The Heritage Foundation
214 Massachusetts Ave. NE, Washington, DC   20002
(202) 546-4400 • fax: (202) 546-8328
e-mail: info@heritage.org
Web site: www.heritage.org

The Heritage Foundation is a research and educational institute dedicated to scholarship, formulation and promotion of conservative public policies. It publishes a variety of position papers and research articles on subjects deemed vital to America's interests and security, such as "Post-Conflict and Culture: Changing America's Military for 21⁰ Century Missions."

Hoover Institution
Stanford University, Stanford, CA   94305-6010
(650) 723-1754 • fax: (650) 723-1687
e-mail: horaney@hoover.stanford.edu
Web site: www.hoover.stanford.edu

The Hoover Institution is a research center devoted to the advanced study of public policy, politics, economics, and international affairs. It publishes the quarterly *Hoover Digest* and *Policy Review*, a newsletter, and special reports, including articles such as "Can Iraq Become a Democracy?" and "War and Aftermath."

The Independent Institute
100 Swan Way, Suite 200, Oakland, CA   94621-1428
(510) 632-1366 • fax: (510) 568-6040
Web site: www.independent.org

The Independent Institute is a nonpartisan research and analysis, scholar-based organization, seeking to foster new and effective directions for the study of governance, and to provide solutions to its problems. The institute publishes *The Independent Review*, a quarterly journal; *The Lighthouse*, a weekly e-mail newsletter, with articles like "Democratic Nation-Building and Political Violence"; and books such as Ivan Eland's *The Emperor Has No Clothes: U.S. Foreign Policy Exposed*—challenging a U.S. policy of preemptive war and nation-building—policy reports, research papers, and the *Independent*, a quarterly newsletter.

Institute for War and Peace Reporting (IWPR)

48 Grays Inn Road, London, UK   WC1X 8LT
+44 (0)20 7831 1030 • fax: +44 (0)20 7831 1050
Web site: www.iwpr.net

The Institute for War and Peace Reporting is a nonpartisan organization that promotes and sponsors initiatives to build and maintain local media in the midst of war, conflict, post-conflict, and reconstruction zones worldwide. IWPR also reports on and analyzes news. Some of its reports include the "Afghan Recovery Report" and the "Afghan Press Monitor."

The Institute of World Affairs (IWA)

1321 Pennsylvania Ave. SE, Washington, DC   20003
(202) 544-4141
e-mail: info@iwa.org
Web site: www.iwa.org

The Institute of World Affairs is a nonprofit, nonpartisan organization founded to foster conflict resolution and international understanding. The Institute provides a variety of programs designed to prevent violence and construct post-conflict peace building. IWA supports seminars, lectures, and publications on conflict resolution, including *IWA e-Newsletters, Investigating Democracy Roundtable Series*, and other reports such as "Political Realities: The Diplomatic Process and Design of Peace-keeping Missions."

International Peace Research Institute, Oslo (PRIO)

Hausmanns Gate 7, Oslo, Norway   NO-0186

+47 22 54 77 00 • fax: +47 22 54 77 01
e-mail: info@prio.no
Web site: www.prio.no

The International Peace Research Institute, Oslo, focuses on scholar research and publications surrounding issues of violent conflict and transformational peace building. PRIO publishes books and articles, including "Building 'National' Armies—Building Nations? Determinants of Success for Post-Intervention Integration Efforts."

International Republican Institute (IRI)
1225 I St. NW, Suite 700, Washington, DC   20005
(202) 408-9450 • fax: (202) 408-9462
e-mail: info@iri.org
Web site: www.iri.org

The International Republican Institute is a nonpartisan, conservative organization promoting worldwide democracy through formation of political parties, civic institutions, democratic governance, and the rule of law. The IRI publishes brochures, newsletters, books, and articles such as "Spreading Democracy Is No Quick Fix, But It's Our Noble Duty," and "Why 'Soft Partition' of Iraq Won't Work."

Middle East Forum
1500 Walnut St., Suite 1050, Philadelphia, PA   19102
(215) 546-5406 • fax: (215) 546-5409
e-mail: info@meforum.org
Web site: www.meforum.org

The Middle East Forum is a think tank working to define and promote American interests in the Middle East. It supports American ties to Middle East democracies such as Israel and Turkey. Publisher of the policy-oriented *Middle East Quarterly*, which includes articles like "Will U.S. Democratization Policy Work? Democracy in the Middle East," its Web site includes articles, summaries of activities, and a discussion forum.

Middle East Institute

1761 N St. NW, Washington, DC   20036-2882
(202) 785-1141 • fax: (202) 331-8861
e-mail: mideasti@mideasti.org
Web site: www.themiddleeastinstitute.org

The institute's charter mission is to promote understanding of Middle Eastern cultures, languages, religions, and politics. It publishes books, research papers, audiotapes, videos, and transcripts from forums it convenes, such as the transcript from "Fractured Realities: A Middle East in Crisis Panel: Reconstructing Afghanistan and Iraq." The institute also publishes the quarterly *Middle East Journal*.

Middle East Media Research Institute (MEMRI)

PO Box 27837, Washington, DC   20038-7837
(202) 955-9070
e-mail: memri@memri.org
Web site: www.memri.org

The Middle East Media Research Institute explores the Middle East through the region's media. MEMRI bridges the language gap that exists between the West and the Middle East, providing timely translations of Arabic, Persian, and Turkish media, and original analysis of political, ideological, intellectual, social, cultural, and religious trends in the Middle East. Its *Inquiry and Analysis* series offers commentary on topics such as, "Iraqi National Congress—an Exercise in Democracy."

Middle East Policy Council (MEPC)

1730 M St. NW, Suite 512, Washington, DC   20036-4505
(202) 296-6767 • fax: (202) 296-5791
e-mail: info@mepc.org
Web site: www.mepc.org

The Middle East Policy Council was founded in 1981 to expand public discussion and understanding of issues affecting U.S. policy in the Middle East. The council is a nonprofit, educational organization that operates nationwide. It publishes the quarterly *Middle East Policy Journal*, which includes articles such as Stephen Day's "Barriers to Federal Democracy in Iraq: Lessons from Yemen."

United Nations Development Programme in Iraq (UNDP in Iraq)
Communications Office, New York, NY   10017
(212) 906-5382 • fax: (212) 906-5364
e-mail: nadine.shamounki@undp.org
Web site: www.iq.undp.org

The United Nations Development Programme in Iraq seeks to help reconstruct the country through three main avenues: democratic governance, economic development and employment, and infrastructure construction. The UNDP in Iraq promotes these three areas through citizen participation in the civic process, gender and human rights building, and utilizing the expertise of Iraqi expatriates to rebuild their country. The UNDP Web site contains reports such as the "Iraq Living Conditions Survey 2004," and "Infrastructure and the Environment," a UNDP strategy to contribute to Iraq's reconstruction through rehabilitating and modernizing the infrastructure.

Bibliography

Books

Tom Athanasiou
and Paul Baer
Dead Heat: Global Justice and Global Warming. New York: Open Media, 2002.

Ronald Bailey, ed.
Global Warming and Other Eco Myths: How the Environmental Movement Uses False Science to Scare Us to Death. Washington, DC: Competitive Enterprise Institute, 2002.

Tim Flannery
The Weather Makers: How Man Is Changing the Climate and What It Means for Life on Earth. Boston: Atlantic Monthly, 2006.

Ross Gelbspan
Boiling Point: How Politicians, Big Oil and Coal, Journalists and Activists Are Fueling the Climate Crisis—And What We Can Do to Avert Disaster. New York: Basic, 2004.

Ross Gelbspan
The Heat Is On: The Climate Crisis, the Cover-Up, the Prescription. Cambridge, MA: Perseus, 1998.

Al Gore
An Inconvenient Truth: The Planetary Emergency of Global Warming and What We Can Do About It. New York: Rodale, 2006.

John Houghton *Global Warming: The Complete Briefing.* 3rd ed. Cambridge, UK: Cambridge University Press, 2004.

Elizabeth Kolbert *Field Notes from a Catastrophe: Man, Nature, and Climate Change.* New York: Bloomsbury USA, 2006.

Jeremy K. Leggett *The Carbon War: Global Warming and the End of the Oil Era.* New York: Routledge, 2001.

Bjorn Lomborg *The Skeptical Environmentalist: Measuring the Real State of the World.* Cambridge, UK: Cambridge University Press, 2001.

James Lovelock *The Revenge of Gaia: Earth's Climate Crisis and the Fate of Humanity.* New York: Basic, 2006.

Mark Lynas *High Tide: The Truth About Our Climate Crisis.* New York: Picador, 2004.

Patrick J. Michaels *Meltdown: The Predictable Distortion of Global Warming by Scientists, Politicians, and the Media.* Washington, DC: Cato Institute, 2005.

S. George Philander *Is the Temperature Rising? The Uncertain Science of Global Warming.* Princeton, NJ: Princeton University Press, 1998.

Barry George Rabe *Statehouse and Greenhouse: The Emerging Politics of American Climate Change Policy.* Washington, DC: Brookings Institution, 2004.

Alan Reed | *Precious Air: The Kyoto Protocol and Profit in the Global Warming Game.* Albuquerque, NM: Green Fields America, 2006.

William Sweet | *Kicking the Carbon Habit: Global Warming and the Case for Renewable and Nuclear Energy.* New York: Columbia University Press, 2006.

David G. Victor | *The Collapse of the Kyoto Protocol and the Struggle to Slow Global Warming.* Princeton, NJ: Princeton University Press, 2004.

Periodicals

Jerry Adler, Karen Breslau, and Vanessa Juarez | "The New Hot Zones," *Newsweek*, vol. 147, no. 14, April 3, 2006.

Tom Bethell | "Truth Be Told," *American Spectator*, vol. 39, no. 5, June 2006.

Edward J. Brook | "Tiny Bubbles Tell All," *Science*, vol. 310, no. 5752, November 25, 2005.

Beverly Darkin | "Long Haul on Climate," *World Today*, vol. 61, no. 12, December 2005.

Stephen J. Dubner and Steven D. Levitt | "The Price of Climate Change," *New York Times*, November 5, 2006.

Myron Ebell | "Love Global Warming," *Forbes*, vol. 178, no. 13, December 25, 2006.

Lauren Etter   "Global Warming: A Cloudy Out-
                      look?" *Wall Street Journal*, December
                      10, 2005.

Josie Glausiusz   "The World Melts and the Masses
                      Mobilize," *Discover*, vol. 28, no. 1,
                      January 2007.

Holman W.   "Decoding Climate Politics," *Wall
Jenkins Jr.   Street Journal*, January 24, 2007.

Clare Kendall   "Life on the Edge of a Warming
                      World," *Ecologist*, vol. 36, no. 5, July–
                      August 2006.

Richard A. Kerr   "Global Warming May Be Homing in
                      on Atlantic Hurricanes," *Science*, vol.
                      314, no. 5801, November 10, 2006.

Jeffrey Kluger   "The Tipping Point," *Time*, vol. 167,
                      no. 14, April 3, 2006.

Bill McKibben   "Energizing America," *Sierra*, Janu-
                      ary–February 2007.

J. Madeleine Nash   "Storm Warnings," *Smithsonian*, vol.
                      37, no. 6, September 2006.

National Review   "Planet Gore," vol. 59, no. 3, March
                      5, 2007.

Fred Pearce   "The Ice Age That Never Was," *New
                      Scientist*, vol. 192, no. 2582, Decem-
                      ber 16, 2006.

Charles W. Petit   "States Take the Lead," *U.S. News &
                      World Report*, vol. 140, no. 13, April
                      10, 2006.

William H.
Rauckhorst

"Energy Ethics," *America*, vol. 195, no. 14, November 6, 2006.

John Collins
Rudolf

"The Warming of Greenland," *New York Times*, January 16, 2007.

Bret Schulte

"Turning up the Heat," *U.S. News & World Report*, vol. 140, no. 13, April 10, 2006.

Kevin Shapiro

"Global Warming: Apocalypse Now?" *Commentary*, vol. 122, no. 2, September 2006.

Peter N. Spotts

"Often Deleted: 'Global Warming,'" *Christian Science Monitor*, January 31, 2007.

Jason Lee Steorts

"Scare of the Century," *National Review*, vol. 58, no. 10, June 5, 2006.

John Stone

"'Global Warming' Scare-Mongering," *National Observer*, vol. 71, Spring 2007.

Jennifer Vogel

"Extreme Weather," *E: The Environmental Magazine*, vol. 16, no. 3, May–June 2005.

Paul Wiseman
and Cesar G.
Soriano

"Worry Flows from Arctic Ice to Tropical Waters," *USA Today*, May 31, 2006.

Daniel B. Wood
and Mark
Clayton

"California Takes Lead in Global-Warming Fight," *Christian Science Monitor*, September 1, 2006.

Fareed Zakaria   "Global Warming: Get Used to It,"
                   Newsweek, vol. 149, no. 8, February
                   19, 2007.

Index